# *Collector's Encyclopedia of*

# *NIPPON PORCELAIN*

## *Fourth Series*

*Joan F. Van Patten*

The current values of this book should be used only as a guide. They are not intended to set prices, which vary from one section of the country to another. Auction prices as well as dealer prices vary greatly and are affected by condition as well as demand. Neither the Author nor the Publisher assumes responsibility for any losses that might be incurred as a result of consulting this guide.

## *Searching for a Publisher?*

We are always looking for knowledgeable people considered to be experts within their fields. If you feel that there is a real need for a book on your collectible subject and have a large comprehensive collection, contact Collector Books.

Cover Design: Terri Stalions
Book Design: Donna Ballard

On the cover:

Top left: Cake set, woodland scene, green mark #47, $475.00 – 550.00.
Top right: Covered urn, 14½" tall, blue mark #52, $1,800.00 – 2,000.00.
Center: Coralene vase, 4¼" tall, mark #243, $550.00 – 625.00.
Bottom left: Moriage flying geese vase, 11¾" tall, blue mark #52, $825.00 – 900.00.
Bottom right: Pitcher, 4½" tall, green mark #47, $550.00 – 650.00.

Additional copies of this book may be ordered from:

Collector Books
P.O. Box 3009
Paducah, Kentucky 42002-3009

@ $24.95. Add $2.00 for postage and handling.

Copyright: Joan Van Patten, 1997

This book or any written part thereof may not be reproduced without the written consent of the Author and Publisher.

# Contents

## Dedication

This book is dedicated to two special friends, Earl Smith and Mark Griffin. Without their encouragement and support this book would never have become a reality. They shared their knowledge and photos, but most of all their friendship.

## About the Author

Joan Van Patten is the author of six other books published by Collector Books, *The Collector's Encyclopedia of Nippon Porcelain, The Collector's Encyclopedia of Nippon Porcelain, Series II, The Collector's Encyclopedia of Nippon Porcelain, Series III, Nippon Porcelain Price Guide, The Collector's Encyclopedia of Noritake* and *The Collector's Encyclopedia of Noritake, Series II.* She has also written numerous trade paper and magazine articles and is a contributor to *Schroeder's Antiques Price Guide.*

She has been on the board of directors of the INCC (International Nippon Collectors Club) since its inception, she served as its first president, and was also the co-founder. She has lectured on the subjects of Nippon and Noritake throughout the United States and Canada. Research, travel, and volunteer work are other major interests of the author.

# Acknowledgments

*"Bees accomplish nothing save as they work together, and neither do men."* Elbert Hubbard

And neither does Joan Van Patten!

An abundance of wonderful photos and information was received from collectors all over the United States. I was overwhelmed with the support and thanks go to all of you. I had so much help that Series V will be following soon after this book!

Collector Books is absolutely the greatest company to work with. Bill Schroeder, Sr. was there from the beginning with the first Nippon book and now his son, Billy, has taken over and is every bit as personable and great to work with as his father. This is my second book with Lisa Stroup, editor at Collector Books and I want to thank her for all her help. With people like these working at Collector Books, is there any wonder it is number one?

I am fortunate to have two special friends who I believe have the finest and most wonderful collection of Nippon in existence. One enters their home and is immediately awestruck by the quality and amount they have accumulated. Stupendous, marvelous, there just are not adjectives to describe this collection. They have amassed a great deal of knowledge about Nippon over the last few years and are kind enough to share their information and photos of their items with readers of this book.

Seventy percent of the photos in this Series are from their collection! They spent two 8-hour days with their photographer taking photographs and then many, many more hours measuring items and noting their backstamps. Their photographer is Clement Photographic Services, Inc. in Ft. Myers, FL. Mark Griffin and Earl Smith used them for *The Collector's Encyclopedia of Noritake Porcelain, Series II* cover shots and readers will be seeing more of Mark and Earl's items which were photographed by Clements in Series V. I think the photography is extra special in this book and much of the credit has to go to these three people.

Mark and Earl also helped with pricing and the chapters on Nippon urns, coralene, and cleaning Nippon items. I think readers are really going to enjoy seeing many pieces of their superb coralene collection.

Earl and Mark approached me about a year ago and suggested that it was time to do another book. They volunteered to have their collection photographed so how could I turn down an offer like that! Thanks Mark and Earl, you're great friends.

Charlene and Elwood Matlosz have amassed a wonderful collection over the years and their daughter Michele took some great photos of their items. Nippon people are always so willing to help. I had run a small ad in the INCC (International Nippon Collectors Club) Newsletter requesting photos for the book. I had anticipated some help but to have someone send you way over 100 photographs, well, I must say I was pleasantly surprised. I only used about half of their photos because I wanted to save some of them for Series V. My thanks go to the Matlosz family for their contribution.

Two special friends, Jess Berry and Gary Graves, are always there when I ask for help with a project and this book was no exception. A number of their photos appear plus Jess's chapter Egyptian Designs on Nippon. Jess also gave me background information on the champion dog series and provided some of the photos for that chapter. Thanks guys for your continued help.

Tony and Nancy Choma wrote a chapter on the airplanes featured on Nippon wares. They've done a lot of research and I know that this information will be savored by readers. They also sent along a number of photos of their wares. These items are not easy to find and today the prices have escalated. Thank you Nancy and Tony for sharing your information.

Lee and Donna Call, friends of mine for many years, sent me photos plus information and old catalog pages from the Manning Bowman Company. Maybe now that readers know what to look for more of these pieces will surface. Thanks go to the Calls for their help.

My friend, Judy Boyd, wrote a chapter on Nippon cobalt pieces. Cobalt is one of my weaknesses and when you check out the first few photographs in this book you'll know why. Judy and I attended the same college at the same time but were not aware of it until we met years later through our Nippon collecting. Nippon has been a big part of my life for many years but the best part of the collecting has been the wonderful friendships I have made with other collectors. Judy, thanks for helping me with this and for your friendship.

Rachel Altounian lives nearby and years ago we used to attend INCC conventions together. Rachel has a talent for detailed research and she has written a chapter on the Dutch influence on Nippon for this book plus more chapters for Series V. Rachel has helped me with other projects and I am grateful to her again. Rachel, you're special, thanks so much.

David Bausch collects items decorated with airplanes, all kinds of items, not just Nippon. But he certainly does have some wonderful pieces of Nippon, too. He sent me information on aerial flight of long ago and also some really great photos of some of his pieces. Thank you David.

Philip Fernkes spent hours and hours photographing Nippon for this book. More hours followed when he did the corresponding descriptions. Phil and Jeanne have a wonderful collection which includes the spectacular molded-in-relief fisherman wall plaque. Phil seems to have mastered his photography skills because the photos I received were really wonderful. Many will be featured in Series V as well. I appreciate all the information that was sent and thank you for sharing your collection with readers of this book.

Lewis and B.J. Longest sent me many, many great photos. Some appear in this book, others will be in Series V but all are of wonderful pieces readers are going to love to see. Lewis also photographed the coralene backstamps for use in this book. Coralene is just one of their passions and once you view the pieces shown in this Series you'll understand why. There's so little of it to be found, demand for it is high and the prices are skyrocketing. Thanks to two special people for your help.

Ed and Joan Vanzo love condensed milk containers — all kinds — but lucky for Nippon collectors they also have many to share with us. A number of them are shown in this book, even more will be in Series V along with information about their decoration. Ed and Joan also collect other wonderful Nippon items and I appreciate that they sent photos of some to me for inclusion in the books.

Bob and Maggie Schoenherr sent me many photos of their collection. It is always so much fun to open up a package and see what other collectors have and this was no exception. Readers are going to enjoy their photos in this book and the next. Lewis Longest was their photographer and as usual did a great job. Maggie and Bob thanks so much for all your help.

I'd like to thank Mark Chervanka, editor of *Antique and Collectors Reproduction News* for all our phone conversations regarding the repros flooding the market. This newsletter is dedicated to informing the public about these types of items and is a must for collectors.

I'd also like to thank my daughter, Wendy, for photographing some of my items and all my reproductions. I feel like the queen of repros because I have amassed such a large collection. I use them in talks to show collectors what not to buy. I think Wendy got to know her Nippon even better once she saw all these pieces.

Reggie Hankin sent some wonderful photos (several will be seen in Series V) and her photographer, Frank Ritter did an exceptional job. I'm sure it was a labor of love for Reggie and I appreciate her help.

I'd also like to thank the many others who helped on this project:

| | |
|---|---|
| Andrea Simone | Kathy Wojciechowski |
| Angelina Simone | Ken Harman |
| David Lucas | Kenneth Landgraf |
| David Przech | Linda Lau |
| Debra Tuttle | Mildred and Olen Stewart |
| Don and Shirley Bakely | Mike and Rosemary Mikolajczak |
| Elmer and Peggy Williams | Scott and Jana Morrison |
| Helen Puckett | Todd and Karen Lawrence |
| Jim and Nancy Powers | |

Thanks to everyone who sent photos and helped with information. I hope you enjoy seeing it all in print.

# Introduction

*"That is a good book which is opened with expectation and closed with profit."* Amos Bronson Alcott

It is my fervent wish that once you've opened this book, read the contents, and viewed the wonderful items that your expectations will be met.

Series IV is a continuation of the other three books in the Nippon series and readers should refer to the first book for color plates numbered 1 – 366, plates 367 – 1210 are in Series II, and plates 1211 – 2378 are in Series III. Basic information regarding Nippon wares will be found in each. I feel that collectors need to study all four book in the series. But please don't just look at the photos. It's also necessary to read the text. Remember, chance favors the prepared mind.

Series IV contains many new marks, an update on the reproduction pieces that are on the market, more pages of old ads, and many chapters full of new information for both collectors and dealers.

As most of you know, good Nippon is becoming more difficult to find. Part of this is due to the degree of sophistication of today's collectors. No longer are they looking for cups and saucers and pickle dishes. I personally think that readers will be awestruck when they see some of the pieces featured in this book. The collection of large vases and urns displayed is mind boggling! Finding and purchasing two or three of these in a lifetime is difficult enough but two of my friends have managed to find well in excess of 100! Many are shown in this book, the remainder will be featured in Series V.

There are also numerous pieces of coralene included in this book. Although most pieces do not bear the word Nippon in their backstamp, they were produced during the Nippon era (1891 – 1921) and qualify for inclusion. These wares are difficult to find, actively sought, and oh so wonderful to own. They glimmer, they shimmer, and make a great addition to any collection.

Nippon prices are soaring right up there with other wonderful wares — R.S. Prussia, Pickard, Limoges. At the top antique shows you will find some spectacular items and generally the price matches the piece. But, there still are some "finds" out there. Keep checking garage sales, estate sales, auctions, and flea markets for that sleeper. Who knows, it could happen for you.

Fads come and go and what's popular one year won't be popular the next. Some collectors think an item is rare if it is an unusual type of ware, say a stickpin holder. Some think a different shape does it or an unknown decor, while others feel that it's a great piece if it's well executed, in mint condition, almost unheard of in Nippon circles, and a fabulous one-of-a-kind item. Many Nippon pieces are difficult to locate, expensive to purchase, and still not rare. There are as many ideas on rarity as there are collectors.

Of course, it's impossible to have everything you want because if this were so you'd be missing the fun known as wanting. But I do believe that there are a few collectors out there who are certainly trying to acquire everything. Possibly it is the quest or chase for the Nippon that is more fun than the actual acquisition. Epictetus once wrote "Things are never so much appreciated as when, like a chicken, we must do a certain amount of scratching for what we get."

As far as prices are concerned they depend upon so many things — which part of the country you are making your purchase, the sophistication of both buyer and seller, the condition of the item, the rarity of the piece. Prices listed for the items shown in all the series are always the most controversial part of the books. No one ever wants to find an item listed for less than they have just paid but they are always thrilled when they obtain a bargain and the price guide lists a value of three times as much. I never do price guides by myself but enlist the help of the top dealers and collectors in the field and there are still big differences in their opinion. Ultimately, I do correlate all their advice and come to what I consider is a fair guide. But it is just that, a guide. It is not intended to set prices but to help collectors and dealers know the approximate price range of a piece.

The following are my rules for collecting:

1. Buy to please yourself! Your collection should reflect your own taste and be for your own pleasure and enlightenment. You have to live with these pieces so buy what you like but buy the best you can afford. Quality items always retain their value.

2. Study, study, study, and study some more. Read the books, talk with other collectors and dealers. Find out why collectors value some items over others. Compare prices. But remember everyone makes mistakes and probably some of my best lessons were learned that way. You will find that some pieces wear well over time and others do not. Our tastes change and evolve over the years. You can always do as most veteran collectors have done, sell off your beginner pieces — one man's trash is another's treasure.

3. Become discriminating — purge that urge to splurge on anything and everything. You do not need one of every type of item ever manufactured. Look for beauty, workmanship, quality, and rarity. Remember to watch for damaged pieces and try to buy items free of cracks, hairlines, chips, etc. Check the handles, finials, and spouts for evidence of breakage. Get to know what the reproductions look and feel like. Buy pieces of sets only if you like the individual item as you may never find the rest of the set.

4. If rules 2 and 3 are too difficult for you follow, go back to rule 1. If you really love an item and can afford it — go for it!

# OLD ADS FOR NIPPON CHINA

## CELERY TRAY.

L6611–12x6¾. Japanese picture decoration. Tokio red embossed edge. 3 in pkg. Each. 39c

## SALT AND PEPPER SHAKERS.

6 salts and 6 peppers. 1 doz. in box. Each with cork.

L5028

L5027

L6181

L5028–2¾x2, spiral column 3 styles floral and gold spray, tinted band edges.. Doz. 33c

L5027–2¾x2, spiral tapering, Japanese decorations. Tokio red top and base... Doz. 36c

L6181–3¼x2⅜, allover Japanese decoration, cobalt top and base, gold ornamented. Doz. 60c

L5025 L5032

L5033

L5025–3⅛ in., tapering column floral decorated, gold tracings, gold traced cobalt blue top and bottom............ Doz. 72c

L5032–3x3⅛, flowers, gold spray, gold traced cobalt blue edge and bottom......... Doz. 79c

L5033–3x2¾, tinted rose decorations, gold traced cobalt neck, gold clouded top. Doz. 89c

## MUSTARD POT.

Each with spoon.

L6190–3x3, ribbed Japanese decoration, Tokio red edge and handles. 1 doz. in pkg........... Doz. 85c

## TOOTH PICK HOLDER.

L1737–Ht. 2¼, vase shape, allover blue and white Japanese decoration. 1 doz. in pkg.... Doz. 25c

## JAPANESE CHINA SALT AND PEPPER SHAKERS.

6 salts and 6 peppers in pkg. of 1 doz. Opening in bottom.

L1730

L2176

L1736

L2182

L1730–2½, allover blue floral print decorations.............................. Doz. 30c

L2176–2¾x1¾, fancy hexagon shape, floral and gold spray decoration, gold clouded top. Doz. 33c

2184

L1736–Chick shape, 2½ in., painted features and feet, natural color yellow shading, with painted wings.... Doz. 39c

L2182–2¾x2, spiral column shape, dainty floral and gold spray decoration, gold traced cobalt blue band top and bottom, gold decorated top. Doz. 45c

L1503

L2184–*Design and price are equally attractive.* Ht. 3⅜ in., tapering column shape, ribbed, floral decorated with gold tracings, wide gold decorated cobalt blue top and bottom edges. Per dozen. 72c

L1504

L1503–3x2¼, low shape, dainty floral and gold spray decoration, gold traced cobalt blue edge and bottom....... Doz. 95c

L1504–3x2¾, tinted luster ground, asstd. rose decorations, gold traced cobalt blue neck, gold clouded and line top. Doz. $1.10

## JAPANESE CHINA VASES.

L1934½

L1780

L1782

L1934½–Pitcher shape, 3⅝ in.. asstd., 3 colors rich yellow, green and cobalt blue, embossed fancy handles. 1 doz. in pkg....... Doz. 39c

L1780–4¾ in., transparent china, beautiful allover blue decoration of landscape, figure and floral designs with birds. 1 doz. in pkg. Doz. 75c

L1782–Ht. 4⅛ in., floral decorations in colors, heavy gold band all around top, gold decorated feet and handles. ½ doz. in pkg. Doz. $1.75

L1784

L2370

L1784–Average 5¼x4, white china, gold decorated cobalt blue feet, neck and handles allover floral decorations, blue band through center solidly outlined and traced with gold. 2 styles. ½ doz. in pkg............. Each, 33c

L2370–Shofu ware, ht. 6¼ in., olive and ground, natural color, strawberry and vine hand painted decoration, gold traced and veined, fancy gold handles and feet, crimped top. 2 pkg. Each, 55c

L2331

L2331–6 in., footed, variegated clouded ground, full blown rose and leaf decoration, raised Moriago decoration in light colors floral and butterfly design, jewel studded, Moriago band edges. 1 in pkg. Each, 69c

L2332 L2333 L2334

L2332–9 in., new fancy shape, daintily tinted ground, full blown 2 color peony and leaf decorations, gold and enamel traced, solid gold handles, beaded and traced, fancy French gold band top and foot. 1 in pkg. Each. 95c

L2333–9¼ in., fancy pitcher shape, Japanese landscape decoration, appliqued Moriago green and white cherry blossom decoration, embossed handle, band top and base. 1 in pkg.............................. Each. $1.10

L2374–Ht. 10 in., fancy shape and decoration, otherwise as L2333.............. Each. $1.15

## JAPANESE CHINA MUSTARD POTS.

L2169

L2170

L2169–3x3, fancy ribbed shape, good quality china, green & blue cherry blossom decorations, open-hand band knot, each with spoon. 1 doz. in pkg.................. Doz. 84c

L2170–3¼x3, dainty rose decorations with gold lace work, cobalt blue knob, side handles and edges, gold tracings...... Doz. $1.25

## MORIAGO VASES.

L2339 L1814½ L2344

L2339–Genuine Moriago. Fancy shape, ht. 5 in., ornamental handles, allover enameled relief decorations in characteristic Japanese figures and floral designs in bright natural colors. 12 in pkg............... Each, 6c

L2340–7¼ in., otherwise as L2339. 6 in pkg. Each, 15c

L1814½–Ht. 8 in., rich dark blended green ground, allover enameled floral decorations, in. border at bottom. ............ Each, 45c

**LARGE SIZE MORIAGO VASE.**

*A rich one to retail at $1.00.*

L2342–12 in., otherwise as S2339. 2 in pkg. Each. 55c

L2365

L2344–Ht. 15, fancy shape, open handles, large hand painted iris decorated on enameled Moriago ground, geometrical design border top and bottom. 1 in pkg. Each, $1.50

L2365–18¼ in., new urn shape, large hand painted peony and leaf decoration with fancy gold scroll, raised enamel, allover scroll and floral ground, geometrical border base, fancy beaded handles, gilt edge..... Each, $3.50

## TOOTHPICK OR MATCH HOLDERS.

L1765

L1739

L1933½ L2172

L1765, Hanging Match Holder–Good size, transparent china, perforation for hanging, corrugated scratcher on bottom, allover blue decorations........................... Doz. 36c

L1739–2 in., ½ vase shape, asstd. hand painted Jap decorations of figures, landscapes and flowers, red band around neck, gold edge. Doz. 38c

L1933½, Toothpick–New shape, ht. 2⅛ in., solid under glazed color, inside and out, asstd. colors........................... Doz. 39c

L2172–2¾x2¼ in., footed crimed top, floral cluster decorations, gold traced edge and feet. 1 doz. in pkg. ................ Doz. 75c

Butler Bros. Catalogs 1906 and 1907

## JAPANESE CHINA SUGAR AND CREAM SETS.

L1584—Sugar 4 in., creamer 2⅞, melon shape, hand painted red rose decoration, light green enamel effect and gold traced drapery, stippled wide gold band edges, cover with gold edge, gold trimmed open handles. Each in pkg.......................................Set, 27c

L2273—Sugar 4x4, creamer 3x3¾, fancy fluted shape, hand painted floral, figure and landscape decorations in colors, panel effect gold and maroon decorated back ground, Tokio red and gold edges and handles. 3 sets in pkg. Set, 27c

L2274—*Note the attractive decorations as well as the low price.* Sugar 4x4, creamer 3½x2¾, fancy melon shape, tinted china, chrysanthemum and leaf decorations with gold lattice, gold decorated cobalt edges and open handles. 2 sets in pkg. Per set, **32c**

L2275—Sugar 4x3¾, creamer 3¾x3¼, fluted melon shape, fancy handles, floral spray decoration with connecting gold scroll work, gold traced cobalt blue edges and handles. 1 set in pkg....................................... Set, 35c

L2276—Sugar 4¾x3, creamer 3¾x3¾, all around shaded floral decoration with gold sprays, fancy cobalt blue edges, handles and knobs, gold traced. 1 set in pkg....Set, 39c

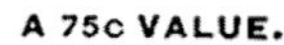

**A 75c VALUE.**

*That will make a splendid leader if you wish to advertise your Jap goods.*

L2286—Sugar 4¾x4, creamer 4½x3¼, ribbed melon shape, white china, allover Japanese figure and landscape decoration, gold illuminated, Tokio red edges, handles and knobs, gold traced. 1 set in pkg. Per set, **39c**

L2281—Sugar 4¾, creamer 3¾, footed urn shape, robin's egg blue good china bodies, large red & white roses, enamel traced, wide beaded gold band top, gold traced feet, fancy handles and knob. 1 set in pkg.......................................Set, 95c

L2283—Sugar 4¼ in., creamer 3½ in., fluted melon shape, full blown pink and red rose cluster and leaf decoration, gold and enamel traced, heavily gold beaded and traced scroll and royal blue edges, gold and blue handles and knob. 1 set in pkg.......................................Set, $1.10

L2284—Sugar 5¾ in., creamer 4¾ in., footed paneled urn, small rose and leaf cluster decoration on delicate pink ground, wide gold beaded and rose panel edges, gold decorated fancy footed handles and knob. 1 set in pkg.......................................Set, $1.35

L1579—Cream 4 in., sugar 4½, low shape, hand painted iris decorations in blue and green, blue decorated handles. Each set in pkg.......................Doz. sets, $2.25

## JAPANESE CHINA 3 PIECE SETS.

Good transparent china, hand painted decorations. Each set comprises teapot, covered sugar bowl and cream pitcher. Each set in pkg.

L1600—Tea pot 5¼ in., creamer 4½ in., sugar 4 in., fluted shape, octagon shape top, hand painted red rose decorations, gold tracing, gold trimmed open handles.........Set, 57c

L2292—Teapot 6 in., sugar 5¼, creamer 3½ in., fine china, artistically decorated with flowers in well blended natural colors and shaded green leaves. Gold traced cobalt blue borders around edges, handles and knobs. Set, 75c

L2293—Tea pot 5x4, sugar 4½x3½, creamer 4x3, ribbed melon shape, allover Japanese figure, flower and lantern decorations, gold outlined, Tokio red edges, handles, knobs and spout.......................................Set, 85c

L1884—Tea pot 5½x5½, sugar 4½x5, creamer 3½x4, fancy footed shape, handled dome covers, wide maroon band handles and knobs, allover Japanese decorations with gold illuminations in paneled effect. Set, $1.72

L2298—Tea pot 6¾ in., sugar 5¾, creamer, 4¼, fancy swell shape, fine white china, allover daintily tinted ground, full blown red and pink rose decoration, enamel and gold traced, wide beaded and gold decorated cobalt edges, gold traced cobalt handles, knobs and spout.......................................Set, $1.95

L2295—Tea pot 5½x5, sugar 1¾x4½, creamer 4x3¾, footed urn shape, fine white china, daintily tinted ground, enamel traced full blown rose decoration, wide beaded French gold edges, fancy gold knobs and handles. Set, $2.00

## JAPANESE CHINA TETE-A-TETE SETS.

L2300—Tea pot 6 in., sugar 4½, creamer 3¾ in., cups 3x1¾, white china, allover Japanese figure and landscape decorations, Tokio red and gold edge, gold decorated handles. 1 set in box. Set, 69c

L2301—Tea pot 5¾, sugar 4¾, creamer 4, cups 3½x2, saucers 4¾, allover rose and forget me not decorations with intermingling gold spray, gold line handles. 1 set in pkg. Set, $1.25

Butler Bros. Catolog 1907

## JAPANESE CHINA TABLE PLATES.

L1919½ — 9 in., allover blue and white printed floral decoration. ½ doz. in pkg. Doz. $1.35

L2384 — 8½ in. Imari ware, fluted sides, scalloped edges, hand painted floral and conventional designs in rich panel border effect, medallion center. ½ doz. in pkg. ............... Doz. $1.50

L1640—9¼ in., Owari, coupe shape, scalloped edge, allover blue and white decoration, wreath center, sprays and bands on outside. ½ doz. in pkg. ............ ............ Doz. $1.50

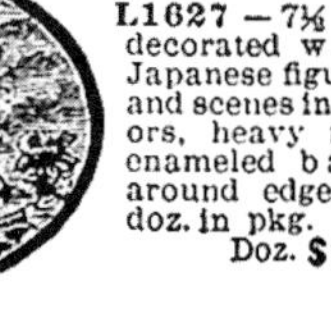

L1627 — 7½ in., decorated with Japanese figures, and scenes in colors, heavy red enameled band around edge. ½ doz. in pkg. Doz. $1.75

L2239—7¼ in. fluted flange, asstd. floral decorations with gold tracings and sprays, gold pink or green edges. Asstd. ½ doz. in pkg. Doz. $1.85

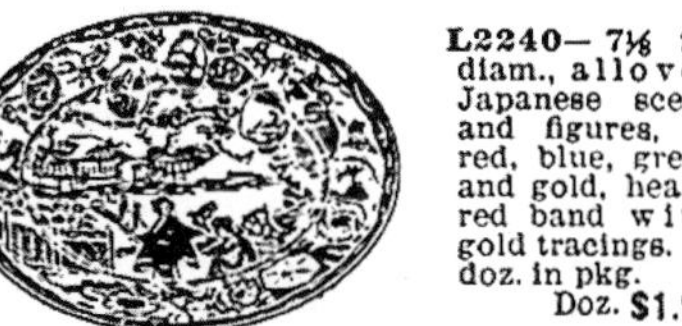

L2240— 7½ in. diam., allover Japanese scene and figures, in red, blue, green and gold, heavy red band with gold tracings. ½ doz. in pkg. Doz. $1.90

L2241—7¼ in., 2 styles, rose and chrysanthemum cluster, natural colors, gold lacework and tracings, deep cobalt blue edge, gold traced. ½ doz. in pkg. Doz. $1.95

L2243—*A low price for such handsome decorations.* Diam. 7¼ in., spiral fluted edge, 2 styles, floral and leaf decoration, enamel and gold traced, gold and cobalt edge. ½ doz. in pkg., asstd. Per dozen, **$2.15**

L2386—8½ in., coupe shape, Imari decoration in panel effect, outside blue spray. ½ doz. in pkg. Doz. $2.18

L2387—8 in. diam., Imari ware, fluted scalloped edge, hand painted colored floral and conventional decorations in medallion effect, 3 floral decorations on outside. ½ doz. in pkg. ....... ...... Doz. $3.50

L2251 — 8¼ in., white china, spiral fluted scalloped edge, luster tinted ground, wild rose cluster decorations, gold decorated cobalt blue border, beaded green inside band. ½ doz. in pkg. ..... ................ ..... Doz. $3.50

L1833 — 7¼ in., octagon shape, large hand painted red and pink American Beauty roses, gold traced green foliage on cream tinted ground, wide cobalt blue border around edges with gold tracings in scroll effect. ½ doz. in pkg.... Doz. $3.75

L1638—8½ in., transparent china, full blown crimson and pink roses with green leaves on tinted background, enamel tracings, embossed gold edge. 2 in pkg. Each, 33c

## JAPANESE CHINA CAKE PLATES.

L2262 — 9 in., deep scolloped shape, rose clusters, panel center with enameled border, rococo cobalt blue edge, gold traced. 3 in pkg. ....... ......... Each, 35c

L1864—8¾ in. 2 color carnation decoration on tinted luster ground, green and gold scroll band frame effect, wide beaded gold flange with maroon and gold panels, gold decorated cobalt edge... ......................... Each, 69c

L1835—10 in. coupe shape, dark green shaded luster ground with rich rose clusters, gold decorated with cobalt blue border, open handle, footed ................. Each, 95c

L1865 — 10½ in., coupe shape, tinted luster center with profuse chrysanthemums, rich colors, heavily beaded gold flange, gold decorated deep cobalt blue border, open handles, footed ................................ Each, $1.00

L2267—10 in., scalloped fluted shape, tinted shadow ground with full blown American beauty and tea rose hand painted decoration, enamel and gold traced, wide beaded and traced solid gold border. Each in pkg. Each, $1.15

## JAPANESE CHINA CHOP DISHES OR PLAQUES.

L1645 — 10¾ in., deep coupe, blue and green rooster, hen and floral decoration. Each, 19c

L1646—11¾ in., characteristic very fancy allover blue decoration in various designs, outside decorations. 2 in pkg. ........ Each, 30c

L2263—10 in., scalloped open work edge, characteristic allover Japanese decoration, panel effect, gold traced, Tokio gold trimmed red edges. Each in pkg. Each, 50c

L2388 — Imari, 12¼ in., scalloped coupe, variegated color decoration with gold in panel effect, wreath center, gold line edge. Each, 50c

L2260 — 11 in., deep shape, fluted scalloped openwork edges. Tokio red and gold trimmed, elaborate Japanese figure and landscape allover decorations, gold illuminated and enameled ................ Each, 75c

L2265—Diam. 11¼ in., deep scalloped shape, openwork edge, gold dotted cream ground, Jap landscape in fan and medallion pattern, wide 3 tone gold traced border. Each in pkg. ................... ........... Each, 95c

Butler Bros. Catolog 1907

**RICH PEONY DESIGNS.**

*Compare prices or better order a sample lot subject to approval.*

**L2360**—19 in. royal blue ground, large shaded peony decorations with enameled petals and leaves, gold decorated open handles with ring and tassel effect, gold band wave top. 1 in pkg. Each, **$2.00**

L2359 L2367

**L2359**—*The new luster bronze decoration.* Ht. 16, royal blue ground, large peony and leaf decorations in shaded bronze outlined with raised gold, gold decorated green band top and base, open handles gold striped. 1 in pkg. Each, **$2.50**

**L2367**—Ht. 16¼ in., fancy tapering shape, hand painted full blown American Beauty roses and leaves enclosed by heavily embossed gold scroll band, rose spray back, royal blue ground, new design, gold decorated handles. 1 in pkg.... ........................Each, **$2.50**

L2362 L2363

**L2362**—19 in. green bronze effect, elaborate [illegible] decoration with leaves.

## JAPANESE CHINA INDIVIDUAL BUTTER PLATES.

L1690 L1695

**L1690**—Diam. 3¼ in., blue and white Sometsuke floral center with neat border. 1 doz. in box.... ........................Doz. **18c**

**L1695**—Extra large round 4¼ in. diam., asstd. floral and rooster decorated center in colors. Doz. **39c**

## JAPANESE "AWATA" VASES.

L1795 L2351

**L1795**—7¾ in., rich red and green backgrounds with large natural colored floral decorations, heavy enamel effect, gold trimmed outlines, fancy tops, gold trimmed edges and handles. 2 in pkg..................Each, **15c**

**L2351**—10 in., asstd. maroon and blue grounds with embossed iris and peony decorations in natural colorings. 4 in pkg......Each, **30c**

L2357 L2355

**L2357**—Ht. 12½, royal blue ground with profuse gold and shaded bronze lotus lily and leaf decoration, green border top outlined with gold, gold decorated openwork handles. 1 in pkg..................Each, **$1.00**

**L2355**—Fancy tapering shape, ht. 16 in., shaded green ground, heavy gold traced iris decorations in colors, side handles. 1 in pkg............Each, **$1.35**

L2356

**L2356**—Footed urn shape, ht. 16 in., deep cobalt blue, large floral and leaf decoration in natural colors with prominent gold outlines and veiling, daintily tinted raised enamel interspersed leaf scrolls, gold band top. 1 in pkg. Each, **$1.50**

**L2232**—6¼ in. all over hand painted flowers, villages, landscapes and figures, gold trimmings, gold trimmed red band around edge. ½ doz. in pkg...Doz. **$1.25**

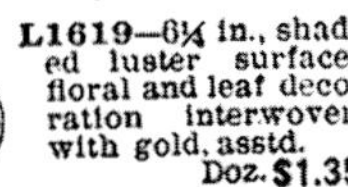

**L1619**—6¼ in., shaded luster surface, floral and leaf decoration interwoven with gold, asstd. Doz. **$1.35**

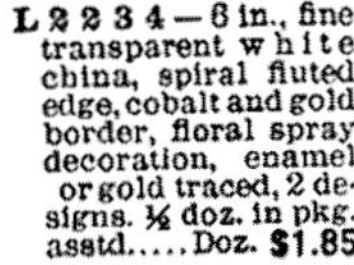

**L2234**—6 in., fine transparent white china, spiral fluted edge, cobalt and gold border, floral spray decoration, enamel or gold traced, 2 designs. ½ doz. in pkg. asstd.....Doz. **$1.85**

**L1832**—5¾ in. octagon shape, hand painted roses on delicate tinted background, gold traced leaves, cobalt blue edge with gold lace work all around. ½ doz. in pkg. Doz. **$2.25**

## JAPANESE CHINA TEA POTS.

All glazed inside.

L1772½ L1775

**L1772½**—Ht. 3½, diam. 4, inside drainer, wicker handle, blue and white, floral and band decoration. 1 doz. in pkg...............Doz. **96c**

**L1775**—Ht. 5½ in., Banko ware, dark brown, allover brown embossed water marked design, 1 in. plain border at bottom, wicker handle, strainer attachment, straight spout. ½ doz. in box...............Doz. **$1.15**

L848 L1773½

**L848**—5 in., fireproof, Kitsu ware, strainer attachment straight spout, white enameled highly glazed body, dark blue allover decorations, wicker handle. ½ doz. in pkg.........................Doz. **$1.45**

**L1773**—Ht. 4½, diam. 4½, as L1772½, but porcelain handle. ½ doz. in pkg.....Doz. **$1.50**

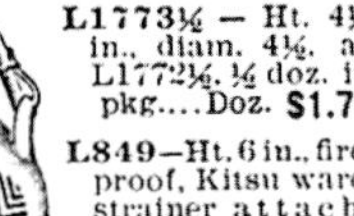

**L1773½**—Ht. 4½ in., diam. 4½, as L1772½. ½ doz. in pkg....Doz. **$1.75**

**L849**—Ht. 6 in., fireproof, Kitsu ware, strainer attachment, straight spout, white enameled glazed body, dark blue conventional decorations, wicker handle. ½ doz. in box. ..Doz. **$1.60**

L849

L2319

**L2319**—4¼x4¾, Japanese figure decorations in panels surrounded by gold traced cobalt blue panel border, cobalt handle, knob and spout. 2 in pkg. Each. **21c**

**L2093**—10 in. hexagon shape, delicately tinted ground, cream to olive, natural red poppy decoration, enamel traced, deep beaded gold cherry blossom border, gold and cobalt lip edge, outside sprays and gold band. Each, **$1.75**

**L2094**—10 in., fine china, wide panel, deep scalloped edge, tinted ground, rose cluster medallion center with maroon and gold border surrounded by rose and conventional panel decoration, heavily embossed and beaded with gold, gold decorated scroll and band edge, outside sprays, gold foot.......................... .....Each, **$2.00**

**L1657**—Extra deep, fluted, diam. 11 in., heavy beaded gold edge, rich shaded green luster flange and center with gold beaded and embossed lace work medallions, rich deep pink rose and gold spray decorations, rose clusters outside, gold line foot........................Each, **$2.25**

Butler Bros. Catolog 1907

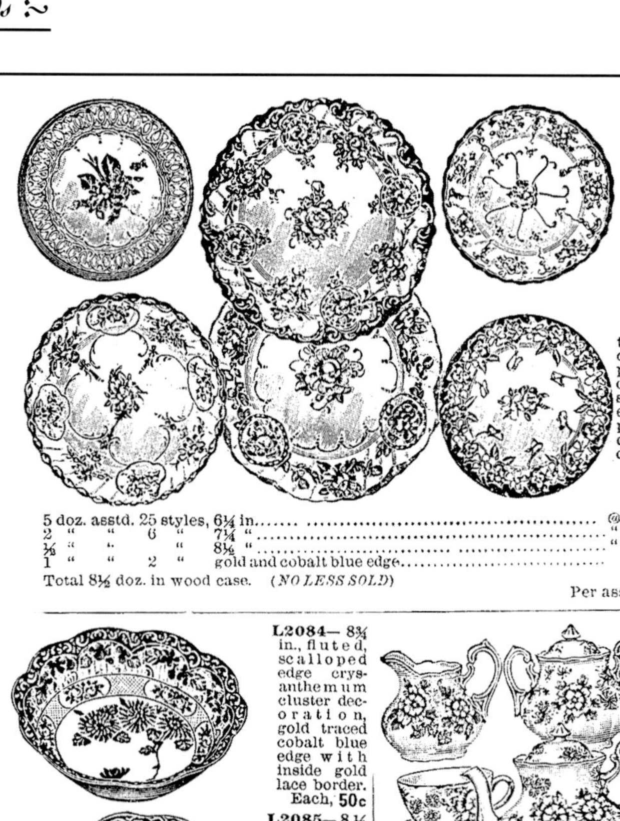

**SPECIAL CASE ASST. JAPANESE HAND PAINTED PLATES.**

L966—All thin transparent china with hand painted floral decorations, gold spray and scroll effects, asstd. plain, fluted, openwork and cobalt blue edge.

| | | | |
|---|---|---|---|
| 5 doz. asstd. 25 styles, 6¼ in. | @ $0 89 | $4 45 |
| 2 " " 6 " 7¼ " | " 2 00 | 4 00 |
| ½ " " " 8½ " | " 2 00 | 1 00 |
| 1 " " 2 " gold and cobalt blue edge | | 3 75 |

Total 8½ doz. in wood case. (*NO LESS SOLD*) Per asst. **$13.20**

L2084—8¾ in., fluted, scalloped edge chrysanthemum cluster decoration, gold traced cobalt blue edge with inside gold lace border. Each, **50c**

L2085—8½ in., footed, scalloped edge, floral and gold cluster decoration, deep rococo blue edge, gold decorated. Each, **57c**

L2083—10 in., butterfly and floral spray decorated ground with Japanese figure and landscape panel decorations, allover gold illuminated, gold traced Tokio red edge, foot and outside spray.......Each, **72c**

L2087—Diam. 10 in., footed, melon shape, heavy gold scalloped edge, allover floral and gold spray decorations, beaded pink or green bands. 1 in pkg...Each, **85c**

L2086—Diam. 10 in., white china, deep footed shape, wide scalloped edge, figure bridge and landscape decoration in natural colors, gold illuminated, gold edge, outside maroon and gold spray, open handles. 1 in pkg.......... ..Each, **98c**

L2090—*A new one of rare merit.* 10 in., white china, fluted scalloped edge, tinted ground, large pink and red chrysanthemum decoration, gold traced and outlined, gold band edge, outside sprays, gold lined foot. Each, **$1.10**

L1612—9 piece, 6½ in. covered tea pot, covered sugar, creamer, 6 cups 3¼ in. and saucers, good china, white body with asstd. natural color floral, gold spray and scroll work decorations, very profuse, almost covering pieces, decorated knob covers and handles. 1 set in pkg. Set, **$1.65**

L2302—Tea pot 6 x 4¼, sugar 5 x 3¾, creamer 3¾ x 3, cups 3½ x 2¼, melon shape, gold cobalt blue feet, knob handles and edges, floral and ornamental gold all around decoration, spray on outside of cups. 1 set in box..........Set, **$1.85**

L2296—Tea pot 4½, sugar 4, creamer 3 in., low fluted shape, tinted cream grounds, red poppy and green and gold fern decoration, beaded gold edges, gold decorated handles. Set, **$1.25**

L2297—Tea pot 4½, sugar 4¼, creamer 3 in., new urn shape, turned-in edges, daintily tinted ground, large pink and red chrysanthemum decoration, enamel and gold traced, gold band edges and foot, fancy gold decorated handles..........Set, **$1.60**

**JAPANESE CREAM PITCHERS.**

L1777

L1758

L1777—4 in., decorated with allover blue, scalloped body and edges. ½ doz. in pkg. Doz. **89c**

L1758—6x4½, white china with allover blue floral decorations. ½ doz. in pkg..Doz. **$2.25**

**FANCY ASSORTMENT.**

*Values that are seldom forced into the 25c range.*

L2035—3⅜x2⅛, saucer 5⅛ in., 1 plain, 2 fancy fluted shapes, in or outside decorations, chrysanthemum wreath, panel and rose and lattice decorations in natural colors with intermingled gold, gold traced cobalt edges and handles. Asstd., ½ doz. in pkg. Per dozen, **$2.25**

**JAPANESE AFTER DINNER CUP AND SUACER.**

*Rapid sellers that more than double your money.*

L1535—Ovide, 2⅞x1⅝, saucer 4⅝, beautiful hand painted allover floral, landscape and figure decorations, rich red band edges. 1 doz. in pkg. Per dozen, **89c**

L837

L2004

L837—Cup 2¼x2⅛, saucer 4⅛ in., fine thin transparent "Sometseka" china, allover blue decorations in floral designs and landscape views. 1 doz. in pkg..........Doz. **85c**

L2004—Cup 2⅛x2¼, saucer 4⅝, floral hand painted decorations, gold trimmings, asstd. blue, green and pink band edges, asstd. 6 decorations. 1 doz. in pkg..........Doz. **92c**

L2007

L2010

L2007—2⅛x2¼, saucer 4½, cylinder shape, transparent china, all over chrysanthemum clusters, gold sprays, colored cloud edges. 1 doz. in pkg..........Doz. **$1.10**

L2010—Cup 2¼x2⅜, saucer 4¾, fluted shape, and asstd. floral decora tions, gilt sprays scroll band, gilt traced edges and handle. 1 doz. in pkg....Doz. **$1.50**

L1522

L1522—Cup 2½x2¼, saucer 4½, fluted floral decorated, gilt band and tracings, pink band edge, gilt traced edge handle. 1 doz. in pkg. Doz. **$1.50**

Butler Bros. Catolog 1907

## JAP CHINA JEWEL, PUFF OR BONBON BOXES.

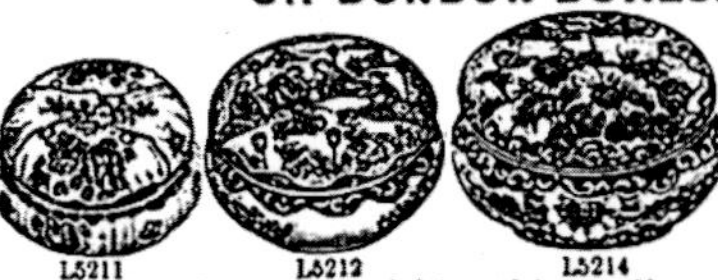


**L5211**—3⅝x2⅛, ribbed, white china, allover floral and leaf decoration, gold traced Tokio red edges. 1 doz. in pkg............Doz. **85c**

**L5212**—4⅛x2⅛, allover Japanese landscape and floral decorations, enamel studded, gold traced cobalt blue edges. ½ doz. in pkg..............................Doz. **$1.25**

**L5214**—4⅜x3, large rose and leaf decoration tinted ground, violet and leaf with gold tracing, gold scroll traced scalloped cobalt edges. Big 25 center. ½ doz. in pkg., asstd. Doz. **$2.15**

L2148

**L2148**—4⅛x2¾, allover Japanese lily and leaf decoration gold veined and outlined, with figure and landscape panel gold, traced cobalt blue edges and base. ¼ doz. in pkg. Doz. **$2.25**

[illegible] 5¼x2¾, waved leaf decorations in colors and gold, ribbon stripe with wide gold decorated cobalt edges. 3 in pkg.............. Each, **25c**

L5215

**L5215**—5x3⅝, narcissus and leaf gold scroll bordered panel decoration, alternating with gold outlined leaves, gold traced irregular edges. 3 in pkg. Each, **27c**

L5216

**L5216**—Diam. 5¾ in., shaded luster ground, delicate violet and leaf decoration in natural colors, embossed gold traced cobalt blue edges. 3 in pkg. Each, **36c**

## JAPANESE CHINA ROSE BOWL.

**L2077**—3⅛x3⅛, cobalt blue feet and crimped edge gold decorated, roses and forget me nots with gold sprays. Asstd. decorations. ½ doz. pkg...Doz. **$2.10**

## JAPANESE CHINA CREAM PITCHER.

**L1755**—4 in., transparent china, fancy allover blue decoration, showing landscape, village and figures, blue trimmed handle. 1 doz. in pkg...............Doz. **85c**

## JAPANESE CHINA AFTER DINNER CUPS AND SAUCERS.

1 doz. in pkg. unless stated.

**L2002**—2x2, saucer 4, allover Japanese decoration, Tokio red and gold trimmed edge.................................Doz. **75c**

**L2004**—Cup 2⅛x2¼, saucer 4⅜, floral hand painted decorations, gold trimmings, asstd. blue, green and pink band edges, asstd. 6 decorations.............................Doz. **89c**

**L1535**—Ovide, 2⅜x1⅝, saucer 4⅜, beautiful hand painted allover floral, landscape and figure decorations, rich red band edges. Doz. **95c**

**L2008**—2¼x1¼, saucer 5 in., small fluted shape, allover hand painted Jap scenery decorations in rich colors and gold, Tokio red under gold edges and handle. ½ doz. in pkg. Doz. **$1.25**

**L2011**—2¼x3⅜, saucer 4½, new fancy shape, fluted, scalloped edge, tinted floral and gold decoration on shaded ground, gold traced fancy cobalt edges and handle. ½ doz. in pkg............Doz. **★1.60**

## JAPANESE CHINA 34 PC. TEA OR LUNCH SET.

**L100** — Good china, popular shapes delicate green edges with gold tracings, allover characteristic Japanese figure and landscape decorations. Set consists of 1 5⅛x4 tea pot, 1 4⅜x4 covered sugar bowl, 1 4x3¼ in. creamer, 1 9¼ in. fluted berry bowl, 6 3¾x2 cups and saucers, 6 4¾ in. fluted sauce dishes, 6 3¼ in. individual butter plates, 6 6 in. bread plates, 6 7 in. table plates. Total 34 pcs. 1 set in case...... ...Set, **$3.75**

## JAPANESE CHINA COVERED HAIR RECEIVERS.

L5223

**L5223**—5¼x3, white china, fancy fluted shape tinted crimson and pink rose decoration with gold spray and edges. 3 in pkg. Each, **33c**

**L5220**—3⅛x2⅛, embossed delicate pink and blue band edges, 2 floral and leaf spray gold traced decorations. 1 doz. in pkg., asstd......................Doz. **89c**

**A BIG VALUE.**

*This special price doubles your profit.*

**L5221**—Average size 3x4⅛, all over Japanese landscape & figure decoration, Tokio red gold traced edges. Asstd. shapes and decorations. ½ doz. in pkg. Per dozen, **$1.50**

## JAPANESE BREAD AND BUTTER PLATES.

1 doz. in pkg. unless specified.

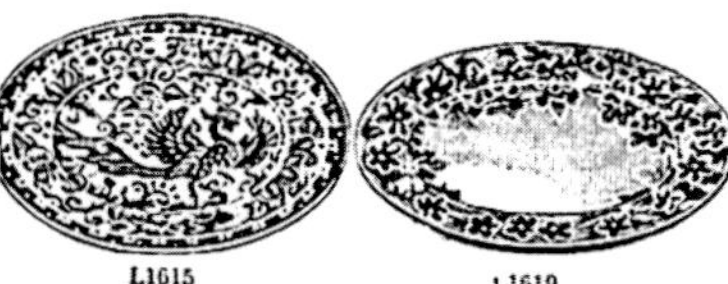


**L1615**—6¼ in., fancy allover blue decorations of birds, dragons, floral and scroll designs. Doz. **72c**

**L1619**—6¼ in., shaded luster surface, floral and leaf decoration interwoven with gold, asstd. Doz. **$1.25**

**A DESIRABLE PROFIT MAKER.**

*Attractive in design and price.*

**L2233**—6¼ in., deep fluted scallop cobalt blue edge gold decorated, allover floral cluster decoration with gold sprays. ½ doz. in pkg. Per dozen, **★1.35**

## JAPANESE CHINA EGG CUPS.

**L5035**—2x2¼ in., footed, clear white china, allover Japanese figured decoration in deep blue. 1 doz. in pkg...................Doz. **25c**

**L5036**—1⅞x2⅛, footed, allover Japanese figure and landscape decoration, Tokio red edge. 1 doz. in pkg.............. ...Doz. **★24**

**L5037**—2¾x3⅛, footed, characteristic allover Japanese decoration in colors, Tokio red and gold edge. 1 doz. in pkg............Doz. **72c**

## JAP CHINA TOOTH BRUSH HOLDER.

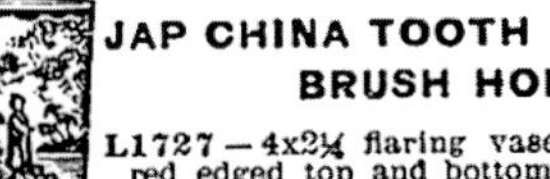

**L1727**—4x2¼ flaring vase, Tokio red edged top and bottom, allover Japanese decoration. 1 doz. in pkg. Doz. **75c**

## JAPANESE CHINA FANCY BONBON OR OLIVE DISH.

**L2131**—5½ in., fluted, Japanese girls, scene and floral decorations in Tokio red and colors with gold illuminations, red and gold scalloped border. ½ doz. in pkg. Doz. **$1.95**

**L2136**—7¾ in fluted deep scalloped, gold traced Tokio red edges, allover Japanese traced decorations gold illuminated in panel effect. ½ doz in pkg. Doz. **$3.00**

## JAPANESE CHINA OATMEAL DISH.

1 doz. in pkg.

**L1744**—5½ in., fireproof, bright blue allover floral decorations. Doz. **72c**

## JAPANESE CHINA BOWLS.

1 doz. in pkg.

**L1740**—4x2¼ in., fireproof allover blue outside decoration, showing birds and flowers, blue band around inner top and bottom..Doz. **45c**

**L1746**—6¼ in., fancy floral designs, allover blue outside decoration, fancy wide blue band around inside edge and bottom. Doz. **89c**

Butler Bros. Catolog Dec. 1908

## JAPANESE CHINA AFTER DINNER CUPS AND SAUCERS.

L1530 — Cup 3x1⅜, saucer 4¾ in., Mino ware china, all over blue decoration. 1 doz. in pkg.................Doz. 42c

L1531—Diam. 3 in., saucer 4¼, low shape white ground, Japanese scenes and figures in asstd. colorings, Tokio red border and handle. 1 doz. in pkg..............Doz. 65c

L2000 — 2 x 2, saucer 4, white china, wreath design floral medallions with gold outlines, colored band edges, gold decorated handle. 1 doz. in pkg........... Doz. 69c

L1534—Cup 2⅛x2¼, Tokio red edge, allover colored Japanese decoration, gold lined handle.. 1 doz. in pkg...............Doz. 85c

L2004—Cup 2⅛x2¼, saucer 4⅝, floral hand paint ed decorations, gold trimmings, asstd blue, green and pink band edges, asstd. 6 decorations..............Doz. 87c

L5005—Cup 3x1⅛, saucer 4⅛ in., thin transparent china decorated in Japanese floral designs with bright colors, gold tracings in scroll effect throughout. 1 doz. in pkg. Doz. 92c

L2007—2⅛x2¼, saucer 4⅛, cylinder shape, transparent china, allover chrysanthemum clusters, gold sprays, colored cloud edges. 1 doz. in pkg. Doz. ★79

### JAPANESE AFTER DINNER CUP AND SAUCER.

*Rapid sellers that more than double your money.*

L1535—Ovide, 2⅜x 1⅝, saucer 4⅜ allover floral, landscape and figure decorations, rich red band edges. 1 doz. in pkg. Per dozen. ★78

L1522—Cup 2⅛x2¼, saucer 4⅛, fluted floral decorated, gilt band and tracings, pink band edge, gilt traced edge handle. 1 doz. in pkg. ...Doz. $1.25

L2009—2¼x2⅛, saucer 4⅛, transparent white china, allover Japanese landscape and floral decoration, elaborately gold illuminated, gold traced cobalt edges and handle. ½ doz. in pkg....Doz. $1.35

L2008—2¼x1¾, saucer 5 in., small fluted shape, allover hand painted Jap scenery decorations in rich colors and gold, Tokio red under gold edges and handle. ½ doz. in pkg.........Doz. $1.40

L2010—Cup 2⅛x2⅝, saucer 4¾, fluted shape and asstd. floral decorations, gilt sprays, scroll band, gilt traced edges and handle. 1 doz. in pkg...........Doz. $1.45

## JAPANESE CHINA AFTER DINNER CUPS AND SAUCERS—Contd.

L2011—2¼x3⅜, saucer 4⅛, new fancy shape, fluted, scalloped edge, tinted floral and gold decoration on shaded ground, gold traced fancy cobalt edges and handle. ½ doz. in pkg............Doz. $1.65

L2012 — 2⅝x2⅛, saucer 4½ in., footed shape, thin white china, tinted chrysanthemum and gold wreath, gold traced cobalt edges and handle, gold tracing and sprays inside. ½ doz. in pkg. Doz. $1.85

L5002—Cup 3⅛x2, saucer 5 in., very transparent china, scalloped ovide shape, cream ground, allover Japanese decoration gold & enameled traced, fancy gold band edge, Tokio red border. ½ doz. in pkg...........Doz. $1.95

L5003 — Cup 2¾x2⅛, saucer 4⅛ in., extra fine china, tall tapering footed shape, allover Japanese landscape, cherry blossom & figure hand painted decoration, gold decorated black & red edges, foot & handle. ½ doz. in pkg.........Doz. $2.25

## JAPANESE CHINA CUPS AND SAUCERS.

L1550—Large size, cup 3¾x2, saucer 5⅛, transparent, rich allover blue print decorations. 1 doz. in pkg. Doz. $1.25

### A NEW OFFERING.

*Staple goods at less than staple prices.*

L1552—Cup 3¾x3, saucer 5⅛ in., thin transparent china, allover Japanese figure and landscape decoration, asstd. green & red, gold decorated edges. 1 doz. in pkg. Per dozen $1.25

L5009—Cup 3¾x2, saucer 5⅛, fine transparent china, 6 floral decorations in natural colors, enameled or gold traced, heavy gold decorated or gold traced cobalt blue edges 1 doz. in pkg., asstd..Doz. $1.50

L2026—Cup 3¾x2, saucer 5⅜, hand painted roses, gold scroll work and tinted edges, gold traced handle. ½ doz. in pkg........Doz. $1.65

L5011—3¾x2, saucer 5⅛, extra quality transparent "Shapin" white china, floral and bird underglazed decorations in delicate green and pink. ½ doz. in pkg..Doz. $1.69

L5016—3¾x2, saucer 5⅛, thin white china, chrysanthemum and forget me not spray decoration gold tracing, gold decorated cobalt blue edge. ½ doz. in pkg..Doz. $1.85

L5015 — Special asst. 3¾x2¼, saucers 5⅛, 3 styles, thin china, fancy fluted and ribbed shapes, 2 inside, 1 outside decoration, butterfly, landscape and panel designs, characteristic Japanese style, elaborately gold illuminated, gold decorated Tokio red edges. ½ doz. in pkg...........................Doz. $1.90

L5020—Cup 3¾ x 2⅛, saucer 5⅛ in., fancy handle, pink and red chrysanthemum and leaf decoration on tinted ground, beaded scroll border, gold trimmed edges and handles ....Doz. $2.25

## JAP CHINA CUPS AND SAUCERS—Contd.

L5017—Asstd. 3 designs, cups average 3⅛ in., saucers 5⅛, fluted, fine thin china, elaborate rose and floral sprays, enamel beading and gold scroll work, cobalt blue, scroll borers, gold edge, blue handles. ½ doz. in pkg. Doz. ★1.95

L5013—Cup 3⅛x2, saucer 5⅛ in., transparent china, richly gold illuminated band painted dancing girl and landscape decoration, characteristic Japanese style, gold traced cobalt edges. ½ doz. in pkg.......... Doz. $3.00

L1856—3¾x2, hand painted floral decoration inside and out, cobalt blue edges and handles, gold leaves and beaded effect around edges. 5¾ in. saucer. 1 in pkg. Each, 50c

## JAPANESE CHINA CELERY OR ROLL TRAYS.

L5259—12 x6¼, open handles, fancy Tokio red edges, all overJapanese figure and landscape decorations. 3 in pkg.. .Each, ★30

L5261—12 x5½ deep boat shape, fancy embossed edge, open handles, allover gold, hand painted, illuminated decoration in Japanese scenes and landscapes, wide beaded gold and enameled floral border in mosaic effect. 1 in pkg................Each, 85c

## JAP CHINA SPOON TRAY.

L5256—9⅛x6, fancy gold & maroon edge with open handles, allover characteristic Japanese decoration in attractive colors. 3 in pkg..........Each, 25c

## JAPANESE CHINA BREAD AND BUTTER PLATES.

L1615—6¼ in., fancy allover blue decorations of birds, dragons, floral and scroll designs. 1 doz. in pkg..........Doz. 67c

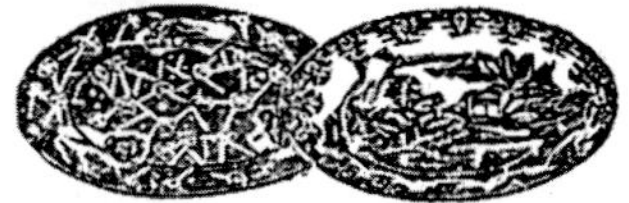

L1616—6 in. thin china, allover blue and white decoration. 1 doz. in pkg.....Doz. 75c

L1617—6 in., transparent china, fluted flange, asstd. 3 Japanese landscape & figure decorations, gold illuminated, red and green edges. 1 doz. in pkg., asstd. Doz. 79c

L5130—6 in., asstd. color edges, floral spray and gold scroll decorations.Doz. 78c

L5131—6¼ in., fluted flange, gold traced red and green edges, 2 gold illuminated geisha girl and floral landscape decorations. 1 doz. in pkg., asstd. Doz. 95c

L2233—6 in., deep fluted scallop cobalt blue edge gold decorated, all over floral cluster decoration with gold sprays. ½ doz. in pkg. Doz. $1.50

Butler Bros. Catolog Dec. 1908

**JAPANESE CHINA TABLE PLATES—Contd.**

**L2387**—8 in. diam., Imari ware, fluted scalloped edge, hand painted colored floral and conventional decorations in medallion effect. 3 floral decorations on outside. ½ doz. in pkg. ............Doz. $3.25

**L1927½**—7⅝ in., fluted sides, scalloped gold edge, hand painted gold trimmed decorations in enamel effects, outside decoration of birds in natural colors. ½ doz. in pkg....Doz. $3.50

**JAPANESE CHINA CAKE PLATES.**

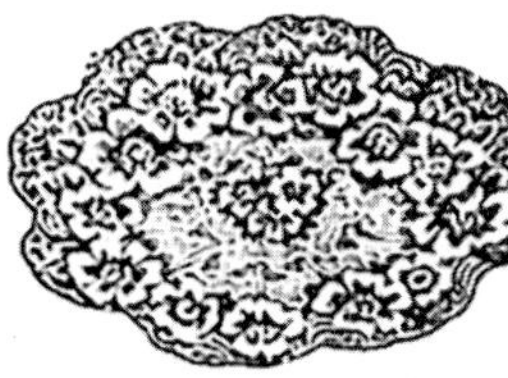

**L5149**—9½ in., fluted scallop edge, coupe shape, enameled beaded center floral and leaf decoration on tinted ground, gold decorated cobalt, band edge. 3 in pkg. ..................Each, 33c

**L5152**—11 in., open handles, new scalloped square shape, tinted ground, floral and leaf decoration, wide irregular gold and cobalt border. 1 in pkg. ..............Each, 65c

**L5154**—11½ in., extra deep, narrow fluted shape, open handles, hand painted enameled beaded Japanese landscape and figure decoration, gold illuminated, gold decorated maroon and green border. 1 in pkg. Ea. 85c

**L1865**—10⅛ in., coupe shape, tinted luster center with profuse chrysanthemums, rich colors, heavily beaded gold flange, gold decorated deep cobalt blue border, open handles, footed...............................Each, 95c

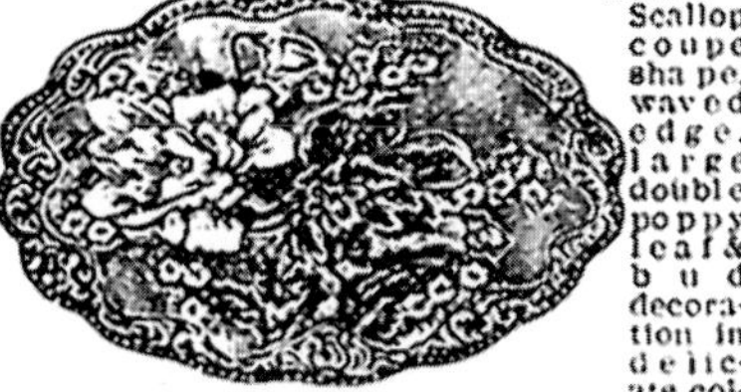

**L5155**—Scallop coupe shape, waved edge, large double poppy leaf & bud decoration in delicate colors with small daisy sprays on clouded green ground, embossed gold border, wide cobalt border. 1 in pkg.........Each, $1.15

Butler Bros. Catolog Dec. 1908

**L5160**—11 in., fancy scallop embossed flange, gold decorated Tokio red edge, alternating black & green gold decorated border ornaments, floral, figure and temple decoration in natural colors and gold. 1 in pkg. Each, 62c

**L5162**—12 in., deep coupe shape, elaborate gold ornamented irregular cobalt band edge, hand painted Japanese landscape decoration in delicate tints, profuse gold tracings. 1 in pkg....................Each, $1.35

**L5163**—12½ in., extra deep shape, irregular embossed gold scroll and beaded gold flange, enamel traced red & pink chrysanthemums and green leaves on tinted ground. 1 in pkg..............................Each, $1.50

**JAPANESE CHINA INDIVIDUAL BUTTER PLATES.**

L1690 L1691

**L1690**—Diam. 3¼ in., blue and white Sometsuke floral center with neat border. 1 doz. in box..............................Doz. 18c

**L1691**—Diam. 3¼ in., Tokio red edges, figure and landscape allover decoration. 1 doz. in pkg..............................Doz. 24c

L1695 L1692

**L1695**—Extra large, diam. 4½ in., Tokio red and blue edges, figure and landscape decoration. 1 doz. in pkg., asstd..........Doz. 39c

**L1692**—3¼ in., deep, dainty and gold sprays in wreath design, gold edge. Asstd. 3 styles. 1 doz. in pkg.........................Doz. 36c

**JAPANESE CHINA INDIVIDUAL NUT BOWLS.**

L5040

L5042

**L5040**—3 in., white china, floral and gold spray decoration, 3 styles, red, green and blue edges, gold ornamented feet. 1 doz. in pkg., asstd. Doz. 36c

**L5042**—3¼ in., wide scallop shape, allover Japanese decoration, green edge, gold ornamented feet. 1 doz. in pkg. Doz. 72c

**JAP CHINA FOOTED NUT BOWLS.**

**L5046**—4½ in., 2 floral and gold spray decorations, variegated color band edges, gold decorated feet. 1 doz. in pkg., asstd. Doz. 89c

**L5047**—*Note the shape and decoration.* 5 in., fluted scallop shape, 2 styles, allover Japanese landscape and floral decoration, gold decorated red and green edges, outside sprays. 1 doz. in pkg., asstd.

Per dozen, **$1.25**

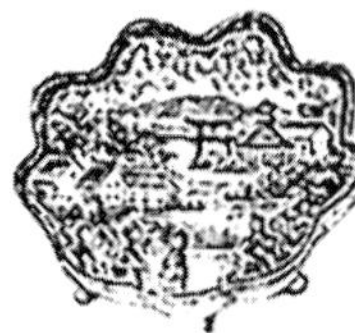

**L5048**—6 in., Japanese landscape and figure decoration, delicate colorings, green border edge, outside sprays, gold decorated feet. 1 doz. in pkg. Doz. $1.75

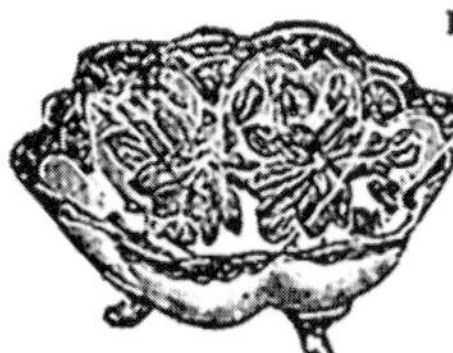

**L5050**—6 in., fancy scallop shape, chrysanthemum and floral spray decoration on tinted ground, gold ornamented irregular cobalt blue edge and foot, outside sprays. 3 in pkg. Each, 33c

**L5054**—6 in., fancy squat shape, ball feet, decorated green and richly gold beaded conventional decoration. 3 in pkg. Each, 50c

**L5056**—8¾ in., fancy flaring shape, fluted, cream ground, gold outlined and beaded floral and leaf decoration, elaborately gold traced cobalt blue edges and feet. 1 in pkg. Each, 72c

**L5057**—8x7, fancy shape, maroon scroll and gold beaded delicately tinted edge, gold ornamented feet, inside gold outlined and enamel traced shaded rose and leaf decoration on tinted ground. 1 in pkg..............................Each, 89c

**L5058**—7¼x7¼, new artistic shape, shaded luster ground, iris and leaf gold traced and enameled beaded violet decoration, gold scroll and beaded border band edge, outside sprays, edge and feet. 1 in pkg..............................Each, $1.25

**L5064**—7¼ in., bowl shape, allover Japanese characteristic figure and landscape gold illuminated decoration, dark green and gold decorated border edge. ½ doz. in pkg..............................Doz. ★1.85

## AIDZU TEA POTS.

Glazed inside.

L1772

L1773

**L1772**—Ht. 3½x4, inside drainer, blue and white flowers and bands. 1 doz. in pkg. Doz. **96c**

**L1773**—As L1772. 4½x4½. ½ doz. in pkg. Doz. **$1.25**

**L6617**—4x3¼. bouquet front and back gold scrolls, small sprays, maroon edges, gold lined knob, handle and spout. ½ doz. in pkg..... Doz. **$1.35**

**L1776** — 5½ x 5¼, inside drainer, allover floral and landscape Tokio red edges, gold traced. ¼ doz. in pkg.....Doz. **$3.75**

## "HANAKO" DECORATED JAPANESE CHINA.

Transparent white china, hand painted combination roses, chrysanthemums and violets with foliage decoration, natural colorings, intermingled gold scrolls and lattice, gold scroll ornamented cobalt blue edges, handles, knobs, etc.

**L6552**, Cup and Saucer—Tea size, 3¼x2, saucer 5½. ½ doz. in pkg. Doz. **$1.80**

**L6553**, 3 Pc. Set — Teapot 5½x4¾, covered sugar 4x4, creamer 4x3. 1 set in pkg. Set. **72c**

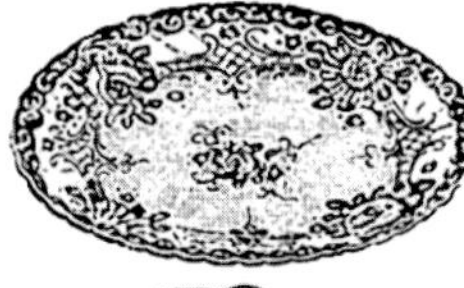

**L6554**, Table Plate—8¼ in., fluted edge. 1 doz. in pkg. Doz. **$2.25**

**L6555**, Table Plate—7¼ in., fluted edge. 1 doz. in pkg. Doz. **$1.75**

**L6556**, Spoon Tray—7¾ x 4¾, open handles. 3 in pkg. Each. **25c**

**L6557**, Berry Set — 10 in. bowl, six 5¼ in. saucers, scallop edge. 1 set in pkg. Set. **$1.25**

**L6558**, Cake Plate—10¼ in. pkg. Each. **50c**

## BREAD AND BUTTER PLATES.

**L1617** — 6 in. fluted flange, Japanese girls and landscapes, colored floral border, Tokio red edge. 1 doz. in pkg..................................Doz. **79c**

## JAPANESE "AWATA" VASES.

L6364 and L6365 — L6381 — L6382

**L6364**—Ht. 3¾, green and yellow cloud surface, hand painted floral and leaf decoration, dark green band edge. 12 in pkg. asstd Each, **3½c**

**L6365**—Ht. 6, otherwise as L6364. 12 in pkg. Each, **8½c**

**L6381**—Ht. 10, graceful shape, new open gold handles, metallic green & yellow allover blending, enamel studded and gold ornamented landscape and marine scene center, prominent gold trimmed and outlined cherry blossom panel base and border top on ribbed antique gold mat, all around design, beaded gold band top and bottom. 1 in pkg. Each, **72c**

L6383

**L6383**—Ht. 12¼, mottled scroll effect brown, cream and terra cotta cloud surface, enamel and gold ornamented large chrysanthemum and leaf branch trailing on embossed gold lattice, all around design, gold ornamented dark green neck and base, fancy gold decorated handles. 1 in pkg. Each, **85c**

**L6382**—Ht. 12½, royal blue body, solid gold embossed leaf and stem framed hand painted flowers and leaves on light tinted surface, floral back, gold ornamented handles. 1 in pkg...... ........Each, **75c**

## TABLE PLATES.

**L1628** — 7½ in., spiral fluted flange, Japanese maids and tea garden. Tokio red edge with gold. Matches **L1553 cup and saucer**. 1 doz. in pkg. Doz. **$1.15**

**L6566** — 7¼ in., fluted, Japanese figures and landscapes, natural colors with gold, gold traced Tokio red edges. ½ doz. in pkg. Doz. **$1.50**

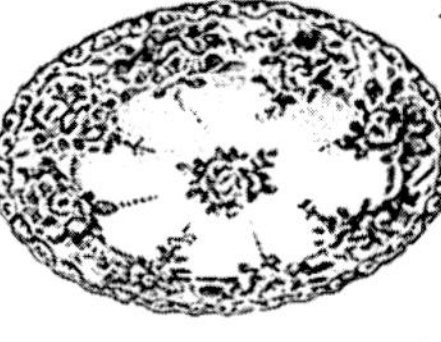

**L6565** — 8¼ in., transparent china, serpentine fluted flange, single and triple floral bouquet border, gold traced, floral center, gold vine cobalt edge. ½ doz. in pkg. Doz. **$2.10**

**L6273** — 7¼ in., white china, twin tinted floral medallions, embossed gold framed ornamental green border, gold band edge. Matches **L6138 cup and saucer**. ½ doz. in pkg................Doz. **$2.15**

## JAPANESE CHINA SUGAR AND CREAM SET.

**L5082**—Sugar 4¾x4, creamer 4½x3¼, ribbed melon shape white china, allover Japanese figure and landscape decoration, gold illuminated, Tokio red edges, handles and knobs, gold traced. 3 sets in pkg. ........ Set. **39c**

## JAPANESE CHINA BERRY SETS.

*Large bowl and SIX saucers to match.*

**L6200** — 8¾ in. bowl, 5 in. saucers, fluted scallop shape, Japanese figure and landscape scene, floral wreath framing, gold ornamented Tokoi red edge...Set. **72c**

**L6203** — 10 in. bowl, 5¾ in. saucers, transparent china, deep flower shape, alternating ornamental framed red rose and floral panel border, gold scroll decorated cobalt blue edge.........................Set. **$1.35**

## CHOCOLATE SETS.

Consists of chocolate pot and SIX cups and saucers. 1 set in pkg.

**L6291** — 9¾ in. pot, cups 2½x2¾, saucers 4¾, paneled, Geisha, landscape and cherry blossoms gold traced, cobalt edges, beaded enamel band, cobalt handle and knob. Set, **$1.50**

**L6293**—Pot 10, cups 2½ x 2¾, saucers 4¾, ribbed column, enamel studded rose and foliage with gold sprays and lattice, gold decorated cobalt blue edges, gold outlined handle and knob. Set, **$1.7[illegible]**

## "SANSUI" DECORATED JAPANESE CHINA.

Transparent white china, Japanese garden, scenic background, floral framing, cobalt blue edges, gold traced.

**L6340, Cup and Saucer** —Tea size, 3¼x2, saucer 5½. ½ doz. in pkg. Doz. **$1.95**

**L6342, Table Plate**—8¼ in. fluted edge. ½ doz. in pkg. Doz. **$2.25**

**L6343, Table Plate**—7⅛ in. fluted flange. ½ doz. in pkg. Doz. **$1.85**

**L6344, Spoon Tray**—7¾x5¼. open handles. 3 in pkg. Each. **32c**

**L6345, Footed Salad Bowl** —10 in. 2 in pkg. Each, **72c**

Butler Bros. Catolog 1910

## JAPANESE CHINA CHOCOLATE POTS.

L7736 L7735

**L7736** — 10 in. paneled, gold illuminated Japanese figure and tea garden, chrysanthemum border, gold ornamented Tokio red edges and handle..............Each, 65c

**L7735**—10 in., fluted lt. green shaded, black outlined tinted wild rose and leaf decoration, decorated spout and cover, gold ornamented cobalt top, base and handle. Each, 72c

## JAP CHINA TEA OR LUNCH SET.

**L101**—Transparent white china, conventional chrysanthemum and leaf decoration, black outlined, gold ornamented, red edges and handles. Set consists of:

1 only teapot, 5x4¼.
1 " sugar, 4x3⅝.
1 " creamer, 3½x3.
1 " 9 in. berry bowl.
6 " cups 3¾x3, saucers 5.
6 " 4¾ in. sauce dishes.
6 " 3¾ in. individual butter plates.
6 " 6¼ in. bread and butter plates.
6 " 8⅛ in. table plate.
Total, 34 pcs. in case..............Set, $4.00

## JAPANESE CHINA BONBON BOX.

**L7823** — 3¼x2¼, rib panels, green tinted gold banded lilac and leaf decoration, green edges...................Doz. 89c

## JAP CHINA HAIR RECEIVER.

**L7821** — 4⅛x3, enamel studded lilac decoration, gold lattice band and scrolls, gold ornamented cobalt edges. ½ doz. pkg. Doz. $2.25


## SALT AND PEPPER SHAKERS.

Each with cork. 1 doz. box, 6 salts, 6 peppers.

L7032 L7742 L6181 L7743

**L7032**—3 in., 2 styles Japanese scene, floral border, Tokio red top and base......Doz. 35c

**L7742**—3⅛ in., allover ground gold ornamented chrysanthemums, Japanese figure medallion front, gold showered top, Tokio red neck.......... .....................Doz. 39c


Butler Bros. Catolog 1912

## SALT AND PEPPER SHAKERS.

Each with cork. 1 doz. box, 6 salts, 6 peppers.

L7032 L7742 L6181 L7743

**L7032**—3 in., 2 styles Japanese scene, floral border, Tokio red top and base......Doz. 35c

**L7742**—3⅛ in., allover ground gold ornamented chrysanthemums, Japanese figure medallion front, gold showered top, Tokio red neck.......... .....................Doz. 39c

**L6181** — 3⅛x2⅛, allover Japanese decoration, cobalt top and base gold ornamented..........Doz. 45c

**L7743** — 3¼ in., octagon paneled clear white, gold framed violet medallions, gold decorated cobalt neck, outlined perforated top, line base..........................Doz. 75c

L7165

**L7165**—3⅛ in., paneled, pastel tints, blossoming cherry trees, gold line neck and base. Doz. 79c

## TEA STRAINER.

**L7848** — 5⅛ in. deep, 3 feet, allover blue & white Sometsuka decoration. 1 doz. in pkg...Doz. 87c

## WELL KNOWN JAPANESE SATSUMA VASES.

Figure decorated fronts, floral backs, panel design, gold outlined beaded, colored band top and bottom, gold ornamented handles and edges.

**L5285**—7½ in., 3 in pkg..Each, 18c
**L5286**—8⅛ in., 3 in pkg..Each, 25c
**L8008** — 9¾ in., 3 in pkg. Each, 35c
**L8009**—12 in., 1 in pkg. Each, 65c
**L5289**—16 in., 1 in pkg. Each, $1.00
**L5290**—18 in., 1 in pkg. Each, $1.75
**L8010**— 24 in., elaborate decoration, profuse gold work, fancy handles, as above.............Each, $5.00

## JAPANESE HAND PAINTED PORCELAIN VASES.

1 in pkg. Decorated front and back.

L8019 L8020 L8023

**L8019**—7 in., pastel tints, gold bead outlined pink and red roses and leaves, beaded gold medallion and scroll border, solid gold edge and handles.........................Each, 65c

**L8020**—9 in., pastel tints, woodland and bird decoration, gold band top and base. Ea., 72c

**L8023**—9⅛ in., gold ornamented marine scene, tan, lavender and ivory tints, beaded gold outlined foliage and violet border, gold top, base and handles..................Each, 95c

## AWATA VASES.

**L8015** —6 styles, ht. 15 in., girth 23 in., dk. green and tan mottled grounds, landscape decorations, sunset effect, enamel studded scrolls and borders, raised enameled birds in moriago effect, ornamented handles. Each, $1.25

## AFTER DINNER CUPS AND SAUCERS.

1 doz. pkg., unless stated.

L7060 L7061

**L7060** — 2⅛ x 1¾, saucer 4¼, allover flowers and figures, enamel traced, Tokio red edges and handle ........Doz. 69c

**L7061**—2¼x2¼, saucer 4, transparent, 2 styles, floral and tea garden scenes, part with green base, Tokio red edges and hdl........Doz. 84c

L7578

**L7578** — Cup 3x2⅛, saucer 5, enamel traced Japanese figure and landscape, Tokio red edge and handle. Doz. 96c

## JAP CHINA CAKE PLATES.

**L7621**—10 in., rib flange, wild rose and leaf wreath, black outlined gold scrolls, gold ornamented scallop cobalt edge. 3 in pkg. Each, 39c

**L7628** —10 in., coupe, embossed edge, all over gold illuminated Japanese tea house and landscape decoration, floral and lantern border..Ea. 65c

**L7632**— 10 in., embossed flange, clear white china, band painted roses, gold outlined brown conventional figure, wide beaded gold band edges and open handles, gold center ornament. 1 in pkg. ...........................Each, 72c

## SUGAR AND CREAM SETS.

**L7761**— Sugar 5⅛, creamer 4⅛, ribbed, lt. blue tint, shaded pink and red chrysanthemums front, back and cover, gold scroll cobalt borders, gold striped hdls. and knob. 3 sets pkg. . ............................Set, 39c

**L7167** —Sugar 5, creamer 4, Japanese scene, gold illuminated, gold decorated borders, Tokio red & gold base, knobs and handles. 3 sets pkg........Set, 39c

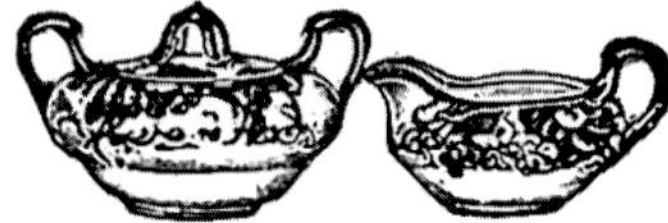

**L7757**—Sugar 6, creamer 5¼, new art shape, lt. blue tint, ripe apple and shaded foliage branches front and back, gold scrolls, wide beaded gold edge, solid gold hdls. and knobs, line feet. 1 set pkg. .........Set, 65c

## FOOTED NUT BOWLS.

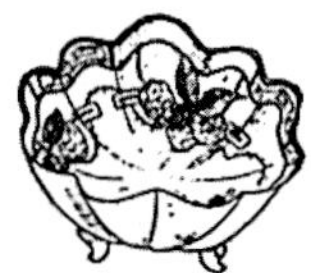

**L9386**—4½ in., ribbed, clear white, strawberry and leaf clusters, green and gold border, gold edge and dec. feet. 1 doz. in pkg......... Doz. **85c**

**L9387**—5½ in., paneled, enamel studded allover Japanese figure and land scape, dk. green edge and feet. 1 doz. in pkg....... ............Doz. Out

**L9390**—7¼ in., rib panels, 3 styles enamel traced hand painted floral decor. gold bands and borders, gold dec. cobalt edge and feet. 3 in box, asstd... .....EACH, **33c**

## FOOTED NUT SETS.

Large dish and six individual bowls.

**L8268**—Dish 5¾, bowls 2¾, allover Japanese landscape decor. Tokio red edges and feet. ½ doz. sets in pkg. Doz. sets, **$2.20**

**L8260**—Bowl 6¼ in., individuals 3⅛ in. ribbed melon, clear white, red and blue grape vine and foliage border, gold band edges, dec. feet. 1 set in pkg...SET, **36c**

**L9239**—Dish 5¼, bowls 2¾, clear white, conventional yellow, lily and green leaf border, beaded gold band, gold edges and dec. feet. 1 set in box....... ...........SET, **50c**

## SALT AND PEPPER SHAKERS.

Each with cork. 6 salts and 6 peppers in box of 1 doz.

L9119 L9120 L6181

**L9119**—3 in., fluted, grapes and leaves, Tokio red edges, gold dec. tops. 1 doz. in box. Doz. **32c**

**L9120**—2¾ in., clear white, 3 styles gold dec. floral designs, gold ornaments, cobalt edges. 1 doz. in box..........Doz. **36c**

**L6181**—3⅛x2⅛, allover Japanese decoration, cobalt top & base, gold ornamented. 1 doz. in box............. ...Doz. **39c**

L9285 L9291

**L9285**—3½ in., fluted panels, clear white, enamel traced pink flower and green stem, enamel ornamented tan bands, gold lined, gold dec. tops. 1 doz. in box. Doz. **45c**

**L9291**—2¾ in., screw top, gold outlined small flowers and leaves, gold scrolls on wide pink band, beaded gold lines, gold dec. top. 1 doz. in box. .... ..... ..... .Doz. **75c**

**L9286**—Aver. 3 in., 6 styles, gold outlined and ornamented conventional floral patterns, beaded gold bands, gold dec. tops. 1 doz. in box, asstd. Doz. **89c**

## MUSTARD POTS.

With spoons.

**L9415**—3¼ in., enamel traced Japanese figures and landscape, bright colors, green edges and knobs. 1 doz. in pkg......Gro. $9 50..Doz. **85c**

**L9416**—3 in., clear white, ribbed enamel traced rose and leaf clusters gold line edges, hdls. and dec. knobs. 1 doz. in pkg................Doz. **92c**

## JAPANESE CHINA BOWL.

**L1741**—5½, footed, allover blue and white decoration. 1 doz. in pkg.......... Doz. Out

## CUPS AND SAUCERS.

**L5007**—Cup 3¾x2, saucer 5⅛, allover characteristic Japanese floral and landscape decoration. Matches L9517 3-pc. set. 1 doz. in pkg Doz. **85c** Gro. **$10.00**

**L9141**—Cup 3½x2, saucer 4¾, pink blossom and green leaf wreath, wide green border under black lattice, green edge, gold line handle. 1 doz. in pkg................Doz. **89c**

**L9129**—Cup 4x2, saucer 5½, blue conventional sometsuke border. Matches L9131 plate, 1 doz. in pkg..........Doz. **95c**

**L9132**—Cup 4x2, saucer 5, clear white transparent china, conventional grapevine border, wide black band, gold line. 1 doz. in box...Doz. **95c**

**L9491**—7¼ in. plate, as L9132 cup and saucer .....Doz. **95c**

**L9146**—Cup 4x2, saucer 5½, enamel traced Japanese figure and landscape design, lt. colors, dk. green edges. 1 doz. in pkg..........Doz. **96c**

**L9145**—Cup 4x2, saucer 5½, clear white transparent, small floral clusters. tan band, red

**L9158**—Cup 4x2, saucer 5½, lt. tan tints, small pink rose and bud clusters, green & gold scrolls, gold edges and inner band, gold line handle and foot. 1 doz. in pkg. Doz. **$1.90**

**L9161**—Cup 4x2, saucer 5½, clear white, small hand painted rose and leaf clusters, black and gold band, gold edges, gold line handle and foot. 1 doz. in pkg. Doz. **$1.95**

**L9167**—Cup 4x2, saucer 5½. ivory tints, hand painted pink rose, gold outlined toned green leaves, gold studded green band between gold lines, gold line foot and covered handle. 1 doz. in pkg..................Doz. **$2.00**

**L9164**—Cup 4x2, saucer 5½, clear white, encrusted gold conventional flowers and leaves, gold scrolls, gold line edges and inlays. 1 doz. in pkg..................Doz. **$2.10**

## AFTER DINNER CUPS AND SAUCERS.

**L1530**—Cup 3x1⅝, saucer 4¼ in., Mino ware china, allover blue decoration. 1 doz. in pkg...................Doz. **45c**

## SALAD OR BERRY SETS.

Consist of large bowl and 6 individual nappies.

**L9665**—Bowl 8¼ in., nappies 4¾ in., clear white pink conventional flower and green leaf border, wide black band, gold edges. 1 set in pkg. Set, **69c**

**L7084**—Bowl 10 in., nappies 5½ in., scalloped allover Japanese figure and floral landscape decoration, Tokio red edges. 1 set in pkg. Set, **75c**

Butler Bros. Catolog 1913 and 1914

## JAPANESE CHINA AFTER DINNER CUP AND SAUCER.

A popular priced seller which will net you 100 per cent profit.

L7188—Cup 2⅞x1⅝, saucer 4⅝. Japanese figure and landscape decoration in bright natural colors, Tokio red band around edges, red enameled handle. 1 doz. in pkg. Doz. 48c

## JAPANESE CHINA OATMEAL BOWL.

A big five center with a large margin of profit.

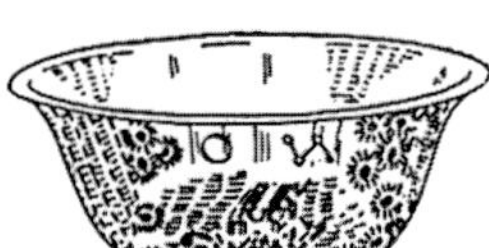

L1741—5½, footed, allover blue and white decoration. 1 doz. in pkg. Doz. 36c

## DOUBLE DECK CHINA EGG CUPS

R5155 R5156

R5155—3⅝ in., glazed white. 1 doz. pkg. Doz. 42c

R5156—Pure white, wide and narrow, gold bands. 1 doz. pkg.......Doz. 69c

## JAP CHINA EGG CUPS.

L5036 L5037

L5036—1⅞ x 2¼, allover Japanese scene, Tokio red edge. 1 doz. pkg. Doz. 33c

L5037—2¾ x 3¼, allover Japanese scene, Tokio red and gold edges. 1 doz. pkg.......... ..Doz. 78c

## CHINA EGG CUPS

R5150 R5151 R5152 R5153

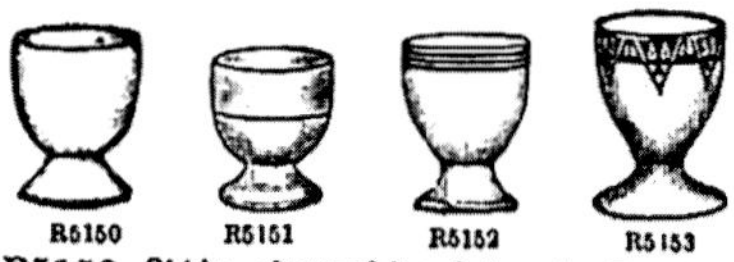

R5150—2¼ in., clear white. 2 doz. pkg. Doz. 15c

R5151—2 in., fillet gold band center. 2 doz. pkg. Doz. 17c

R5152—Clear white, 3 gold bands, 1 doz. pkg. Doz. 25c

R5153—2⅜ in. wide, 3 fillet gold band, base. 1 doz. pkg..........................Doz. 36c

5007—3¾x2. saucer 5¼, allover characteristic Japanese figured and landscape decor. Matches L5008 plate. 1 doz. in pkg.................Doz. 98c

9142—3¾ x 2, saucer 5¼, plain white translucent china, suitable for decorating. 1 doz. in box.......Doz. $1.08

·670—3¾ x 2, saucer 5¼, inted cluster rosebud & foliage wreath, cobalt edges and se, gold stripe handle. 1 z. in box.........Doz. $1.10

6—3¾x2, saucer 5¼, clear transparent china, ma- d on edges and han- doz. in pkg. Doz. $1.15

L4702—Cup 3⅞x2, saucer 5¼, vari-color art floral border, dark green edges, gold stripe hdl. 1 doz. in box. Doz. $1.25

L4062—3⅞ x 2, saucer 5⅝, clear, white translucent china, gold band edge, inner and base lines, gold stripe hdl. 1 doz. in box. Doz. $1.20

L4683 — 3⅞ x 2, saucer 5¼, enamel traced pink & lavender wild flower wreath, green and gold foliage, enamel studded gray band, gold edges and stripe hdl. 1 doz. in box. Doz. $1.25

L4671—3¾x2, saucer 5¼, pink, blossom & green foliage wreath, gold edge, festooning and stripe hdl. ½ doz. in box.................Doz. $1.25

L4676—3¾x2, saucer 5¼, vari-colored oriental floral border, gold edges and stripe hdl. 1 doz. in box..........Doz. $1.35

L4677—3⅞x2, saucer 5¼, blue block border with pink rose buds & entwined foliage, gold edges and stripe hdl. ½ doz. in box .............Doz. $1.40

L4697—3¾x2, saucer 5¼, gold traced pink & blue blossom panels, fancy gold edges, inner band and stripe hdl. ½ doz. in box.......Doz. $2.50

## JAP CHINA TABLE PLATES

L5008—7¼ in., allover characteristic Japanese figure and landscape decor. Matches L5007 cup & saucer. 1 doz. in pkg...............Doz. 98c

L5297—7¼ in., large wild rose spray, bright colorings, fancy green edge. 1 doz. in box. Doz. $1.15

L4684 — 7¼ in., enamel traced pink & lavender wild flower wreath, green & gold foliage, enamel studded gray band, gold edges. 1 doz. in box................Doz. $1.25

## JAP CHINA SALT AND PEPPER SHAKERS

1 pc., hole in bottom for filling, each with cork. Equally assorted salts and peppers.

L5077 L5085

L5077—3¾ in., Geisha girl and landscape, gold dec. top and scrolls on cobalt bands. 2 doz. in box................Doz. 39c (Total 78c)

L5085—3¼ in. paneled, enamel traced trailing berry vines, light blue neckband, gold dec. top and base line. 2 doz. in box.................Doz. 48c (Total 96c)

L5082—6 styles, aver. 2¾ in., gold traced floral and conventional border designs, gold beadings, dec. tops and base lines. Asstd. 1 doz. in box...................Doz. 92c

## CHINA TOOTHPICK HOLDERS.

R5147 R5148

R5147—2¼ in., paneled, flower embossed, 2 styles, pink or green luster, yellow or pink roses. 1 doz. pkg., asstd. ...........Doz. 35c

R5148—2¼ in., terraced, embossed, shaded green luster, pink roses. 1 doz. pkg. Doz. 42c

## TOOTHPICK HOLDERS.

L8195 L8198

L8195—2⅜ in., flower and butterfly decor., blue bands, Tokio red edge...... ..Doz. 32c

L8198—2¾ in. hand painted large red roses and green leaves, gold stems, gold ornamented cobalt edges and foot. Doz. 87c

## HAND PAINTED PORCELAIN VASE ASSTS.

L5220—6 styles, 7⅛x 8¼ in. pastel tints, 2 water scenes 2 landscapes 2 floral decors., gold traced and beaded borders, edges and hdls. 1 doz. in case, 35 lbs.............Doz. ★4.50

L5228—12 styles. 7 to 9¾ in., pastel tinted grounds, gold outlined, floral and art landscape and marine scenes, gold art enamel traced, conventional borders and handles. 1 pr. each style. Assd. 2 doz. in case, 60 lbs...........Doz. $6.00

Butler Bros. Catolog 1914 – 17

## 7 PC. CHOCOLATE SETS

Each set consists of covered chocolate pot and SIX cups and saucers.

L2266—Pot 9½ in., 6 cups, 2⅝x3, saucers 5 in., fancy Japanese tea garden decoration, variegated colors, red edges, gold loops, red handles. 1 set in pkg. SET (7 pcs.), **$1.50**

L749—Pot 9½, 6 cups 2¾x2½, saucers 4¾, paneled, trailing pink roses and foliage sprays connecting gold floral bands, brown striped nile green edges, gold decor. edges, hdl. and knob. 1 set in pkg. SET (7 pcs.), **$1.95**

L7262—Pot 9½, 6 cups 2½x2¾, saucers 4¾, paneled, embossed dec. ivory tinted border, white enamel traced wild roses and foliage, gold band edges, handles and knobs. 1 set in pkg....SET (7 pcs.), Temp. Out

L6209—Pot 9½, 6 cups 2½x2½, saucers 4¾, gold and enamel traced red & yellow peonies with green leaves front and back, gold decorated matt green border, gold beading, edges and decorated handles. 1 set in pkg....SET (7 pcs.), **$2.25**

L7261—Pot 9½, 6 cups 2½x3, saucers 5, paneled gold outlined blue border inner rosebud band, gold dec. edges, handles and knob. 1 set in pkg....SET (7 pcs.), **$1.50**

L1040—Pot 8½, 6 cups, 2¼x2¾, 6 saucers 4¾, white china, lt. blue border, inner gold line rosebud and foliage band, gold decorated edges, handles and knob. SET (7 pcs.), **$2.75**

L6199

L6206

L6205

L6199—Pot 9¼, SIX cups, 2¾x2¾, saucers 5, pink & blue blossoms in gold framed panels, ivory tint border, large center spray, gold edges and striped hdls. 1 set in pkg......SET (7 pcs.), T. O.

L6206 — Pot 9, 6 cups 2¾x2¾, saucers 5, ivory tint border with gold traced flowers, blue band and butterflies, gold dec. tinted handles, knob and beaded edges. 1 set in pkg SET (7 pcs ), **$2.50**

L6205—Pot 9¾, 6 cups 3x2⅝, saucers 5, hexagon paneled, gold outlined conventional pink and yellow floral sprays, foliage, latticed and barred ivory bands with gold beaded edges, gold decor. edges, hdls. & knob 1 set in pkg SET (7 pcs ), **$2.50**

## SALT & PEPPER SHAKERS

L7444—2½ in., floral and lattice design, red band, green dec. top. 1 doz. in box..............Doz. ★32

L5907—3 styles, 2½ in., gold dec. cobalt edges, floral sprays, gold dec. tops. Asstd. 1 doz. in box.....Doz. 42c

L7445—3¼ in., garden landscape, gold decorated top and scroll on cobalt bands. 1 doz. in spaced box......Doz. 48c

## CHINA INDIVIDUAL SALT DIP

L6459—1½x1, gold edge and inner wreath, gold dec. feet. 2 doz. in pkg.....Doz. 42c (Total 84c)

## CHINA CONDIMENT SETS

L6394—3 pcs., salt, pepper and toothpick holder. In display box with cut-out, characteristic stenciled band with blue and red flowers, red edge band, gold lined tops, each set in box. 1 doz. sets in pkg....Doz. sets, **96c**

L716-1—Covered cheese and cracker tray, attached covered cheese container 1⅝ x 4¼, white china, trailing wild rose decor., gold dec. knobs and edges. 1 in pkg. Each, ★69

L716-2 — Covered cheese and cracker tray, attached covered cheese container 1⅝x4¼, white china, pink rose and peony decor., gold dec. knobs and edges. 1 in pkg.......... ......Each, ★69

## 7 PC. AFTER DINNER COFFEE SETS

L7626—7 pcs., pot 8¼, 6 cups 3¼x2¼, saucers 5⅛, Japanese landscape, Tokio red edges, handles, spout and knob. 1 set in pkg. SET (7pcs.), Temp. Out

L7630—7 pcs., pot 8½, 6 cups 3¼x2⅝, saucers 5⅛, allover landscape, green enamel studded and traced, brown edges, handles, spout and knob. 1 set in pkg. SET (7 pcs.), Temp. Out

## 7 PC. SALAD OR FRUIT SETS

Each set consists of one large and SIX fruits.

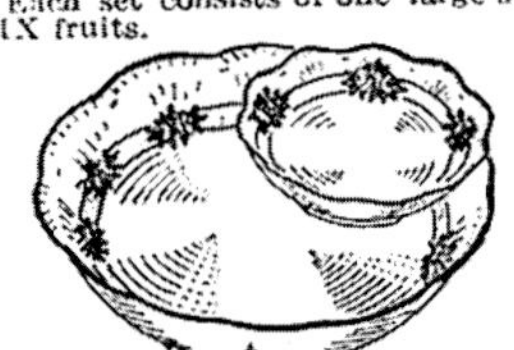

L6372—Bowl 8½ in., SIX nappies 5 in., ½ in. gray and brown band with pink floral rosettes, green edge and band. 1 set in pkg. SET (7 pcs.), **75c**

L7171—Bowl 8¾ in., 6 fruits 4½ in., floral spray in gold lined paneled effect, pink, gold edges. 1 set in pkg............SET (7 pcs.), **98c**

L745—Bowl 10 in., SIX fruits, 5½, hexagonal, large roses and foliage on tinted ground, gold paneled border. 1 set in pkg. SET (7 pcs.), **$1.25**

## 7 PC. NUT SET

L6330—Dish 6 in., SIX indvs. 3 in., white luster, purple violets, green leaves, with long stems, gold edge. ½ doz. sets in pkg. Doz. sets. **$4.00**

## 7 PC. FOOTED NUT SET

L7332—Bowl 5½ in., SIX indvs. 2¾ in., alternating pink floral medallion in gold lined paneled effect. ½ doz. sets in pkg. Doz. sets. **$4.50**

## AFTER DINNER CUP AND TRAY SET.

For serving tea and toast, chocolate and cake, etc., also for invalids.

L9430—Cup 2¾, tray 8¼, ivory tint enamel traced pink cherry blossom and green leaf border, gold edges, 11 hdl. and foot. 3 sets in bo Set, ★

Butler Bros. Catolog 1918 and 1919

## *Sources Discovered*

What are the sources of the decoration we find on our Nippon wares? The techniques used? Many, of course, were original designs but some were direct copies of paintings that were popular at that time period. The Japanese were imitative as well as innovative. They saw what was popular in the United States and catered to our taste. They were definitely influenced by the fashion of the day.

The Japanese copied the Royal Bayreuth tapestry vases and the English Wedgwood. They were also influenced by the style of decor used on Rookwood, R.S. Prussia, and Gouda wares.

We find cartoon and poster art, Dutch, English, Egyptian, and Russian scenes, Scottish castles, Venetian gondolas, Roman chariots, Bedouins, knights in armor, biplanes of the era, and old touring cars.

Some of the novelty pieces feature animals reminiscent of those used on Royal Doulton items. Many of the dolls were copied right down to the stickers, Happifats, Jollikid, Kewpie, Manikin, Baby Bud, and even Little Red Riding Hood from the fairy tale.

We do know that many items had original designs, the majority of which were created in the United States by artists working for the Noritake Co. Old salesmen's sample pages show us some of the artists' original hand-painted watercolor drawings.

We also find a few pieces that incorporate Japanese themes; Geisha girls, Japanese garden scenes, and villages but, by and large, the majority of the designs were to please the American and European markets.

Some sources are found accidentally. One day while I was visiting the Brandywine River Museum in Chadds Ford, PA, I looked up and spotted a painting which is also found on a Nippon piece. A look through some of the museum's other works and a second was found. This museum contains many of W.C. Wyeth's (1882 – 1945) paintings. *In the Crystal Depths* was painted in 1906. It's an oil on canvas, 38" x 26" and was used as an illustration for the series "The Indian In His Solitude." It was featured on the cover of *Outing* magazine, June 1907. *The Hunter* circa 1906, painted by W.C. Wyeth is an oil on canvas, 38⅞" x 26⅝" and was used as the cover illustration for the June 1906 issue of the *Outing* magazine.

Frederic Remington, another famous artist, also had his work copied on Nippon pieces. Remington (1861 – 1909) was an illustrator, painter, and sculptor. His field sketches were often done in watercolor and he is known for his paintings of soldiers, cowboys, Indians, and toughs. He also produced drawings for the *Outing* magazine in his career.

In 1905 he painted one of his most popular prints *Coming to the Call* which was a continuation of his 1901 *Calling the Moose*. It was published as a full-color double-page for the August 19, 1905, *Collier's Weekly* spread. It was later offered in the 1906, 1907, and 1910 *Collier's* catalogs and in 1908 it was advertised as one of Remington's four best paintings. It was also featured in an edition of 25 art pictures representing the best works of America's greatest artists published by *Collier*. On the Nippon pieces this print was copied almost faithfully except that on some of the wares there is not a moose shown but birds of some type.

*Shadows at the Water Hole* was featured in the August 24, 1907, issue of *Collier's Weekly*. It was published as a full-page spread and later offered in *Collier's* catalogs in 1907 and 1910. In 1908 it too was advertised as one of Remington's four best paintings. In this print he provides us with vibrant colors and hints at the action to come. The original print has three Indians, two horses, and a blanket. Nippon artists varied their scenes somewhat from the original.

*The Collector's Encyclopedia of Nippon Porcelain* reference numbers are:

*In the Crystal Depths*, plate 735

*The Hunter*, plates 123 & 722

*Shadows at the Water Hole*, plates 740 and 2620

*Coming to the Call*, plates 126, 730–734, 738–39, 741–42, 1902

Our majestic eagle found in plate 1470 is found on an old Audubon print.

The Indian chiefs we find on Nippon wares can be identified by checking history books. Sitting Bull can be located in plates 125, 128, 2616, 2618. Chief Joseph is on items in plates 723, 725, and 727. Red Cloud is found in plates 128, 1584, 1906, 2617, and 2618.

Most of the Indian portraits are decals and are displayed as a medallion on the item. Some of the portraits are surrounded with applied moriage trim of crossed arrows and the staff of power which is entwined with tosseled rope and buffalo horns.

Our Indian Chief series depicting Sitting Bull, Red Cloud, and Chief Joseph show all wearing medals awarded to them by the United States government as a means to pacify the Indians and encourage them to turn to farming.

During President Ulysses S. Grant's term (1869–1877) the medal given to the Indian chiefs featured President Grant on one side and a globe surrounded by farm implements on the reverse. The front side of the medal bore the bust of President Grant within a wreath of laurel and also bore a calumet and a branch of laurel. The words "United States of America, Liberty, Justice and Equality, Let Us Have Peace" are printed on it.

On the reverse side is a globe resting on farm implements (rake, shovel, etc.) of industry with the Bible above it and rays behind it, stars going around the edge. The words that appear are "On Earth Peace, Goodwill Toward Men."

Sitting Bull was born around 1834 and died on Dec. 15, 1890. He was a Sioux headman and shaman. He was described as six foot tall with a well-formed head and splendid face. He was considered one of the most honest, able, and idealistic statesmen in Indian history.

He bore scars from taking part in the famous Sun Dance performed by the Sioux. To show his bravery he sacrificed approximately one hundred pieces of flesh. The skin of Sitting Bull was pierced with a skewer. Long rawhide leather straps were tied to this skewer and also to a pole. Sitting Bull had to pull until his flesh gave away. He went without food or water for three days. He could not cry out for his courage and endurance were being tested.

Sitting Bull is probably best known for organizing Indians to fight in the Battle of Little Big Horn. The result was the massacre of several hundred Army troops and General George Custer in 1876. After the battle Sitting Bull retreated to Canada but was forced to return in 1881.

In 1885 he toured with Buffalo Bill's Wild West Show. He joined to get more food and help for his people. He stayed for one year and Buffalo Bill (William F. Cody) gave him a parting gift of a horse that could do tricks.

He was shot when Indian police attempted to arrest him in 1890 for reintroducing the Ghost or Sun Dance to his reservation.

Chief Red Cloud was an Oglala Sioux chief and a man of great courage. He was called "as full of action as a tiger" by one U.S. general.

Red Cloud's War is counted as the only one that the Indians won against the United States. After this he kept his word to live in peace. He went to Washington for the medal he received from President Grant and is shown wearing it in old photos. In 1870 Red Cloud gave an address to an audience of whites about the wrongs perpetrated against his people. He told them that his advice to his followers was "If you wish to possess the white man's things...you must begin anew and put away the wisdom of your fathers, you must lay up food and forget the hungry, when your house is built, your storeroom filled, then look around for a neighbor whom you can take advantage of and seize all he has." Chief Red Cloud died in 1909.

Chief Joseph, 1840 – 1904, was a member of the Nez Percé tribe. His Indian name was Thunder Rolling Down from the Mountains. He was one of the most famous chiefs in Indian literature and was referred to as a red Napoleon. He learned to read at an early age at the Christian Mission School. He preached forbearance, "Better to live in peace than to begin a war and lie dead."

The tribe's Nez Percé name originally came from Frenchmen (before the time of Lewis and Clark) and stands for pierced noses because they once wore ornaments in their noses.

In 1877 the Nez Percé tribe surrendered and Joseph reluctantly agreed to go to the reservation. He is known for saying "I am tired of talk that comes to nothing. It makes my heart sick when I remember all the good words and all the broken promises." He died in 1904 supposedly from disillusionment and a broken heart. His surrender speech regarding the great suffering of his fellow Indians at the hands of white men is unforgettable. "I think that, in his long career, Joseph cannot accuse the Government of the United States of one single act of justice."

*In the Crystal Depths*

*In the Crystal Depths*

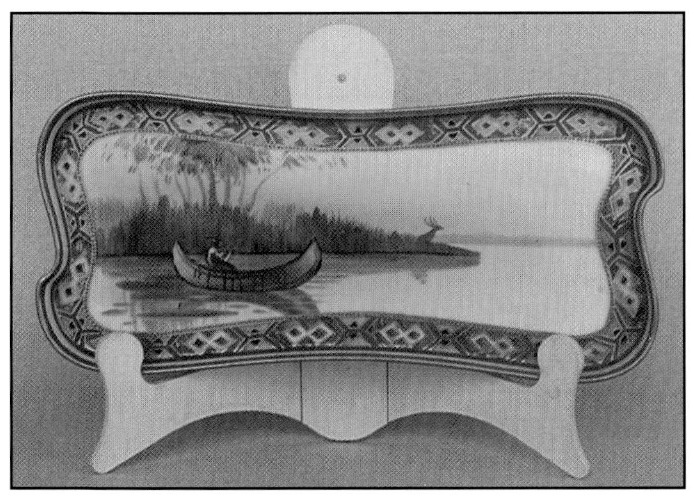

*Coming to the Call*, pin tray, 8¾" long, 3¾" wide. Green M in wreath.

*Coming to the Call*, fruit compote, 10" across, 4½" high. ¼" blue maple leaf mark.

*The Hunter*

*Shadows at the Water Hole*

Chief Sitting Bull

Chief Sitting Bull

Humidor, Chief Joseph, green mark #47, 5½" tall.

Humidor, Chief Red Cloud, green mark #47, 5¾" tall.

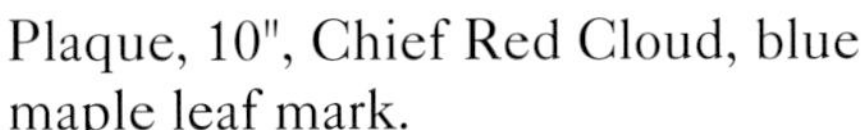

Plaque, 10", Chief Red Cloud, blue maple leaf mark.

Champion dogs can also be found on some of our Nippon items. The champion dog series is found on 10" plaques, 7" whiskey jugs, 5½" tall humidors, 5½" long cigarette boxes, 5" round ashtrays, and 6½" ashtrays with matchholders. All these pieces have a cream ground with brown and rust geometric designs except the jugs which have a marbled background. The dogs are featured in a panel or reserve. To date all that have been found have been backstamped with the green M in wreath #47 mark dating their production between the years of 1911 and 1921.

The English bulldog breed was developed in England in the thirteenth century. They were known for their courage and ferocity in the sport of bullbaiting. Bullbaiting became illegal in 1835, and the dog was then bred to eliminate viciousness. Today's bulldogs are even tempered, affectionate animals in spite of their ferocious appearance. Mature male dogs weigh about 50 lbs., the females about 40. The bulldog has a massive head, wide shoulders, and short, stout and straight forelegs. It has a large, broad nose and a deep, broad, and full chest. The dog's lower jaw projects, enabling the dog to take a grip that is difficult to break. In 1875 bulldog breeders formed the Bulldog Club, Inc. which is still in existence.

The name can be found at the bottom of some of the decals while it seems to have been cut off on others.

The four dogs are named:

Champion L'Ambassadeur (white in color), he was the first American bred champion in 1896.

Champion Katerfelto (white with dark spots), owned by C.G. Haptons.

Champion Rodney Stone (dark brown with a white chest), owned by Walter Jefferis.

Champion Bromley Crib (brown with white nose band).

L' Ambassadeur

Katerfelto

Rodney Stone

Bromley Crib

Wall plaques.

Humidors and whiskey jugs.

Cigarette box.

Ashtray with match holder.

## Around the World with Nippon Porcelain

The Noritake Co. had its artists paint porcelain wares in all kinds of styles and patterns, whatever would appeal to the public. After all, the name of the game was sales.

Some day sit down and take a really close look at your Nippon items. You can travel all over the world. From Bedouin campsites to Venice, Italy, to the pyramids of Egypt or perhaps a quick trip to Holland or a rocky cliff hideaway. It's all there — all you have to do is look!

# *Egyptian Designs on Nippon*

***by Jess Berry***

For centuries the Western world has had a love affair with things Egyptian which on occasion resulted in an outpouring of Egyptian decor, styles, music, dance, etc. Even architecture had an "Egyptian fling" as evidenced by a church built in Sag Harbor, Long Island, in 1844, entirely of wood, termed Carpenter's Egyptian, which vaguely resembled the formal pylon of the Ptolemaic temple at Edfu, dedicated to the god Horus. There were also stone structures built in the Egyptian mode featuring columns composed of several plant-based styles with lotus flower capitols. Unfortunately, many of these structures in the United States have lost the race with so-called progress and are no longer standing.

Since Napoleon's famous foray into Egypt, museums in France, England, America, and Egypt (to name a few) have amassed huge collections of Egyptian artifacts. With so much interest, is it any wonder that Nippon also had its day in the Valley of the Nile? After all, Nippon was meant for a Western-world market and Egyptian decorated items sold readily. "Egyptian" Nippon covers a wide range of scenes from pyramid and palms, to the purely stylized god or goddess which will be the focus of this feature.

Of particular interest is a bowl which copies the jeweled pectoral of Pharaoh Rameses II (see Fig. 1). This marvelous piece combines three animals symbolic of royal power, the falcon, the vulture, and the sacred cobra. It is remarkable how closely the design was copied, including the symbols in the cartouche listing the Pharaoh's name. Even the colors used on the Nippon bowl are a close approximation of the original pectoral.

The round trivet and mug are a depiction of Anubis, the jackal-headed god of the dead (see Fig. 2), while the ladies shown on the pair of trivets and ashtrays represent the goddesses Isis and Ahmose (see Fig. 3). The figure wearing the sun-disc headdress depicted on the small ashtray closely matches a tomb painting of the god Horus (see Fig. 4).

The square humidor is of interest as it has the appearance of a canopic chest used for storage of jars holding various organs of the dead during mummification rites. The hexagonal humidor features stylized lotus flowers which figure so prominently in the art and architecture of ancient Egypt (see Fig. 5).

Another theme popular on Nippon is shown on the matching candleholders (see Fig. 6). This is a diverse assortment of items in Egyptian style showing four seated gods (sons of Osiris) around the bottom along with various hieroglyph-type symbols, and depicts a scarab or sacred beetle in the center of the design. Ancient Egyptians considered the scarab to be connected with protecting the heart of the dead, thus insuring a source of life and movement in the afterlife. This design is also found on both large and small vases, however to date I haven't discovered it on humidors.

Some of the most impressive Nippon pieces with Egyptian-style decor are those done in molded relief. The humidor has three figures in high relief, a pharaoh and his queen seated, the falcon-headed god standing, and a winged scarab crowning the lid (see Fig. 7). The body of this piece is decorated with incised hieroglyph-type symbols. This humidor is found in two colorations; dark shaded brown with rich brushed gold highlighting, and cream ground with brown definition.

Both the inkwell and box (see Fig. 8) have the cream ground with shaded brown trim. The inkwell features a seated pharaoh grasping royal and devine scepters in his hands on both the front and reverse side of the piece, which is unusual as on most Nippon items the reverse face is less detailed. On the lid in molded relief is the scarab, this time with folded wings. The lid of the box depicts a kneeling figure playing a harp and the bust of pharaoh wearing the crown of Lower Egypt. Both of these pieces, like the humidor, have incised hieroglyph-style symbols and lotus flowers as well as much raised geometric fret work.

Unique among the molded Egyptian pieces is an 8½" candlestick formed like a temple column. The shaft is incised to resemble cut stonework with carved symbols; the top molded to represent the lotus flower capitols so often found in Egyptian temple architecture; and the base features a series of leaves and a delightful row of incised designs marching around the edge. On the shaft of the column in bold relief is a full-figure standing pharaoh again wearing the crown of Lower Egypt and holding a royal scepter. This item also has the cream ground with trim and accents done in shades of brown.

As a group these four pieces are superb and represent molded relief Nippon at its very best.

Egyptian-type Nippon offers a wide source of interest and sheds light on the tastes of that era. Had the tomb of Tutankhamen been discovered a few years earlier there would probably have been other even more spectacular Nippon Egyptian representations.

Figure 1.

Figure 2.

Figure 3.

Figure 4.

Figure 5.

Figure 6.

Figure 7.

Figure 8.

# *Dutch Influence During the "Nippon Years"*

***by Rachel Altounian***

There are obvious Dutch influences present on various Nippon porcelain pieces. These influences show us the true Japanese talent for copying what was foreign to them in their desire to learn about the Western world. The most prevalent are windmills; either painted in detail in the foreground (V.P. plate 1603), set amongst thatched roof cottages and tranquil horizons (V.P. plate 934) or painted in the distant background of the ships in harbor scenes (V.P. plate 1052 right). Also painted are men and women in Dutch clothing (V.P. plates 235, 933, 990, 999). The Gouda style (V.P. plate 142) is imitative of a Dutch technique rather than a theme.

As early as 1605, trade between Holland and Japan was well established. The Dutch East India Company had a trading post in Deshima (Nagasaki), an easily accessible port. Delft porcelain was shipped to Japan and Japanese porcelain was shipped to European markets. Japan also traded actively with the Portugese, who in 1542 were the first Europeans known to be in Japan. Along with Portugese traders came Jesuit missionaries who successfully established Christian communities in Japan. By 1614 the number of Japanese Christians had been estimated to be one million. The Shogunate, or military dictator, at this time, Ieyasu, grew suspicious of the Christians and launched a series of persecutions. By 1638, all Christians, both Japanese and Portugese, were executed and Portugese trade had ceased. Ieyasu believed the Dutch would not influence the traditional feudal society, so they were allowed to continue trade under a watchful eye.

Thus, the "Closed Door" years began, and Japan's only contact with the West was through the Dutch trading station. Chinese traders had limited rights at Nagasaki under strict supervision. British and Russian ships attempted to establish trading rights but failed. Japanese scholars learned the Dutch language and translated literature as well as medical, astronomical, and scientific works. Some scholars suffered arrest and persecution for doing so until Shogun Yoshimune relaxed edicts against foreign books and learning in 1716.

In the years that followed, Japanese curiosity for Dutch culture and Western society grew. By the late 1800s the assimilation of Western techniques was very evident in literature, art, and sciences. The Japanese were slowly opening their eyes to the promise of the new Western way of life which they felt would eliminate the worsening socioeconomic state caused by a decaying feudal society.

By looking beyond the obvious Dutch themes on Nippon porcelain and by studying the works of Dutch painters of the seventeenth century, there are similarities. V.P. plates 865, 870, 871, and 873 are reminiscent of the vivid still lifes of the seventeenth century Dutch painters. Ships in harbor scenes were also a favorite theme with the Dutch masters. Curiously, Nippon scenes of ruins (V.P. plates 854 and 1043) resemble innumerable paintings of ruins done by Dutch artists who resided in Rome. Nippon landscape scenes with richly hued horizons illuminated by the warm glow of sunlight are borrowed from Dutch seventeenth century landscape paintings. It seemed as if the Japanese copied the subtle use of light from the Dutch masters. A famous Japanese scholar, mathematician, and ship captain, Honda Thshiaki (1744 – 1821), who was concerned with the economic strengthening of Japan through Western ideals, praised Dutch realistic paintings and denounced Japanese renderings of landscape. This is proof that Dutch paintings did enter Japan, for there would be no other way for this scholar to see them.

Each Nippon piece is a hand-painted work of art. Learning about historic events preceding and during the Nippon years helps one understand why certain themes and styles were used.

Imitative of Gouda wares.

Reminiscent of still lifes of Dutch painters.

Bowl with a windmill design.

# Airplanes

*by Tony and Nancy Choma*

Why airplanes on Nippon? What caused an interest in the early 1900s? America looked upon aviation as entertainment, a kind of vaudeville in the sky. England and France realized their potential and were keenly interested in the new flying machines. Taking into account the two types of airplanes that are pictured, we offer the theory that two major events in 1909, the first crossing of the English Channel and the Reims meet, lead to the Nippon airplanes. Both events were highly publicized and brought worldwide attention to aviation. Newspaper pictures of the airplanes helped spread the word.

By mid-1909 French airplane builders were closing the gap in aviation development between America and Europe, which was revealed by Wilbur Wright's stunning 1908 flights in France. An energetic, hawk-nosed manufacturer of automobile headlights, Louis Bleriot, began to occupy himself passionately with problems of aviation.

France soon took the lead in pre-World War I aviation, providing a homegrown hero, Louis Bleriot, who crossed the English Channel on July 25, 1909. The Bleriot XI, in which Louis Bleriot won immortality for his cross-channel flight, used many design improvements including wing warping. Bleriot had built his original monoplane in 1897; although he steadily perfected the design in subsequent models, the No. XI monoplane in which he set out from Calais was still a frail, unproven aircraft. Bleriot poured his own and his wife's fortunes into his experiments, and by October 1908 had achieved some slight success, using wingtip ailerons for control.

The tiny machine had first appeared at a Paris exhibition in December 1908. At 4:35 a.m. on July 25, 1909, Bleriot, suffering from a burned foot and without so much as a compass in his pocket, headed his little monoplane into the air heading for England. Bleriot's flight demonstrated great courage; the 37 minutes it took was about as long as his frail 25hp 3-cylinder Anzan engine had ever run without stopping.

Covering the 25 miles across the Channel in 37 minutes, he collected both the *Daily Mail's* $5,000 prize and a $2,500 prize from a wine company, and became the first man to fly across a stretch of water from one nation into another, as well as attracting extraordinary publicity around the world. After Bleriot's landing in England, H.G. Wells said, "...in spite of our (naval) fleet this is no longer, from the military point of view, an inaccessible island."

The design of the Bleriot XI was interesting in that it incorporated many features that we have since come to take for granted in airplane design: monoplane wings, tractor propeller directly attached to the engine crankshaft, hinged tilting stick and rudder pedal controls, and a covered fuselage structure. Bleriot had now become the chief foe Glenn Curtiss would have to face at the Reims meet in August 1909. The actual Bleriot XI may be viewed at the Smithsonian Institution Air & Space Museum in Washington, D.C.

Glenn Curtiss started out building bicycles, as did the Wright brothers, then became a record-setting motorcycle racer and a creator of powerful, lightweight engines.

The Reims meet, the Grande Semain d'Aviation de la Champagne of August 22 – 29, 1909, offered huge prizes and attracted 38 aircraft, about evenly divided between biplanes and monoplanes, of which 23 flew. Among the entries, nine were Voisings, four Bleriots, four Antoinettes, four Henri Framans, six Wrights, a Breguet, and a Curtiss, which was an update of the Golden Flyer.

The moth-like monoplanes had captured the popular imagination, and after Bleriot cut some fancy capers, the American's chances looked slim. During the week French aviators kept chalking up records and smashing up airplanes. Curtiss counted 12 planes on the ground wrecked or disabled. All the flyable airplanes existing in the United States did not number a dozen.

On the last day Curtiss set a record of 15 minutes, 50 seconds, average speed 46½ miles per hour. Bleriot waited until just 20 minutes shy of the closing gong to make his last try to beat the new record. Curtiss was sure that Bleriot would win and was already discussing building a faster plane. All of a sudden the U.S. flag went up the staff and the band began to play "The Star Spangled Banner," Curtiss had won by 6 seconds.

Newspapers promptly proclaimed Curtiss, Champion Aviator of the World. The honor did not last long, as records were toppled fast in those days.

Both of these events are commemorated on many works of Nippon art such as plaques, trinket boxes, cups. It is interesting to note that most of the pieces are small in size and devoid of gold ornamentation. Also for the most part the aircraft are quite technically accurate considering that the artist probably worked from newspaper pictures.

In the early phase of our collecting airplane pieces we found very few examples and they were generally low in cost since they had no gold ornamentation. Recently we have not been able to find any greater abundance of pieces but have seen a significant increase in price due to their rarity.

# *Aerial Flight Portrayed on Nippon Porcelain*

*by David K. Bausch*

"Aerial flight is one of that class of problems with which man can never cope," so said the noted astronomer, Simon Newcomb in 1903.

I am sure that most people in 1903 agreed with Simon, if God had wanted man to fly he surely would have given him wings!

At least two men thought differently, Wilbur and Orville Wright. While most people felt the air was reserved for the birds, Orville and Wilbur were busy building their first flying machine in their bicycle shop.

After their successful flight at Kitty Hawk, backyard aeronauts started to build their own flying machines. The age of flight had arrived.

It wasn't long before artists and craftsmen were busy making images of some of these flying machines. Nippon porcelain was no exception. Early aircraft was featured on many different china items made in Nippon and other countries.

It is difficult to identify any of the aircraft, for like so many artists of the day, they never actually saw the real thing. Consequently the flying machines do not look exactly like one make or the other, but they do have some similarities to planes made by: Wright, Voisin-Farman, Santo-Dumont, Levavasseur Antinonette (or in any combination of the above).

Wall plaque, 7½" wide.

Hanging ferner with ram heads, 3½" tall, green mark #47.

Double hanging matchbox holder, 5" tall, mark #47.

Toothpick holder, 2" tall, green mark #47.

Covered box, 4" wide, mark #47.

Covered box, 3" wide, mark #47.

Covered box, 3½" wide, mark #47.

Heart-shaped covered box, 2¾" wide, mark #47.

Nappy, 4¼" wide, mark #47.

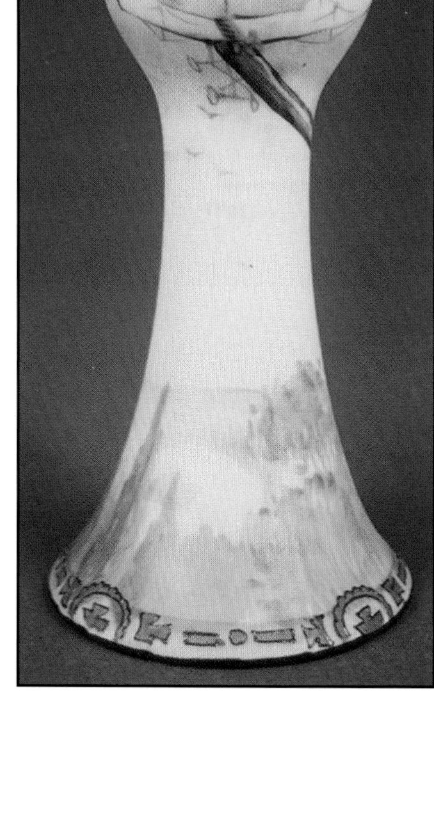

Open hatpin holder, 4¾" wide, mark #47.

Small vase, 2¾" tall, mark #47.

Loving cup, 6" tall, mark #47.

Footed vase, 4" tall, mark #47.

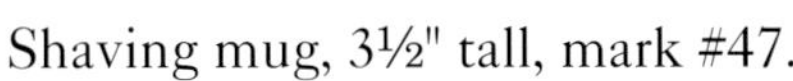

Shaving mug, 3½" tall, mark #47.

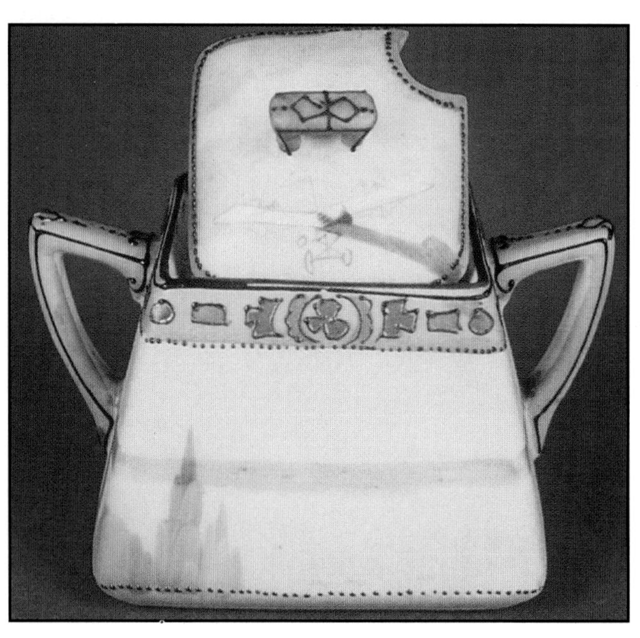

Mustard pot, 2½" tall, mark #47.

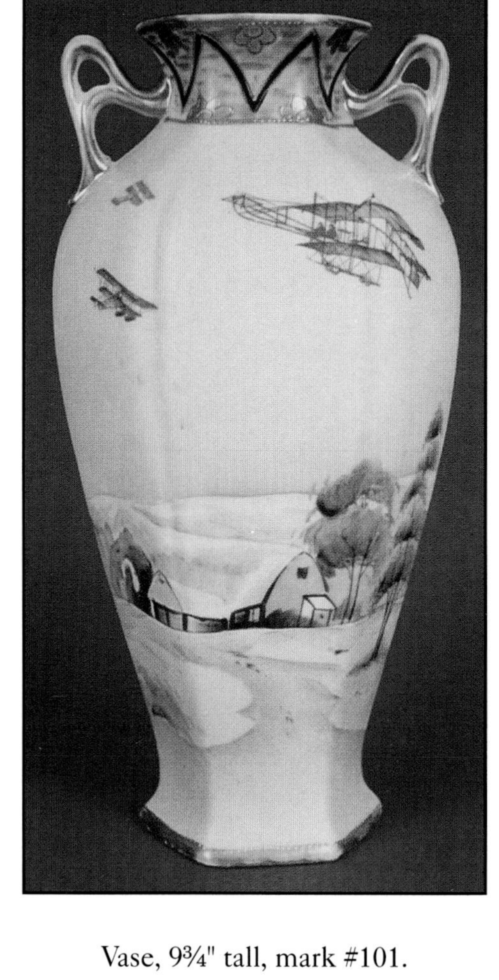

Vase, 9¾" tall, mark #101.

Vase, 7¾" tall, mark #99.

Pitcher, 4" tall, green mark #47.

Demitasse cup and saucer, saucer is 4¾" wide, green mark #7.

Trivet or tea tile, mark #47.

How one collector displays his items.

# *Nippon Coralene*

*by Earl Smith*

As you will note as you view the wonderful Nippon items featured in this book, coralene is but one of the beautiful decorating styles that emerged from Japan during the Nippon era. It is uncertain when the production of coralene began, but we know from previous research done by Joan Van Patten that Alban L. Rock, an American living in Yokohama, Japan, applied for the patent to register his invention on August 19, 1908. The patent was granted on February 9, 1909, and mark numbers 242, 243, and 244 reflect this patent number. The history of the patent numbers of marks 245 and 246 is uncertain at this time as they are not U.S. patents for porcelain and, therefore, must be patent numbers from other countries. We can logically assume that the production of coralene began around 1909 thus placing coralene in the middle of the Nippon years, 1891 – 1921.

The photographs displayed in this series show the wide variety of decorating styles which utilized coralene. From exquisite portraits to lush florals and scenics to bold geometrics, there is a design to suit every Nippon collector. Common to all is the process used to produce each style. This process is described in detail in Alban Rock's patent application reproduced at the end of this chapter. This information should be studied to better understand the decoration we all admire and to further appreciate the amount of time required to produce coralene wares. Of particular interest, is the fact that the color of coralene comes not from the glass beads but from the fusing medium upon which clear glass beads have been placed. Therefore, the artist created his design not with paint as on the majority of Nippon items, but with a colored fusing medium. This must have been more difficult especially for items showing subtle shading such as the bleeding heart flowers and leaves on the vase in plate 2525. By more closely examining each piece of coralene, one gains a better appreciation of the amount of time it must have taken to produce just one piece. You will also note that most coralene items have a matte background finish to highlight the brilliant reflective quality of the glass beads. However, some have a gloss finish in addition (plate 2534) which is yet another style of decoration. Still others utilize cobalt blue which produces a striking contrast (plate 2567).

On many pieces, the coralene decoration constitutes the entire decor (plate 2503). On others, it is simply used as a decorative trim design to enhance another decorating style such as a portrait (plate 2501) or a hand-painted scene (plate 2533). Some collectors feel that the more coralene on an item the better. However, I would suggest that the overall decoration should be viewed to determine desirability. An allover coralene decor may not be as attractive as another item which utilizes coralene only as a decorative accent. Sometimes more is not necessarily better. Of course, as in any collecting field, personal taste determines all.

There are three major art styles found on coralene. The most common is Realism which predominates the earlier Nippon era. This is shown in the Victorian-inspired floral decoration of plates 2503 through 2507. The second major art style is Art Nouveau with its curvilineal elements and asymmetric design. This influence is seen in plates 2511, 2533, 2551. The third major style is one inspired by the arts and crafts movement which began in England in the latter part on the nineteenth century and worked its way to America. This design was a rebellion against the cumulative influence of man's changing taste over the centuries and focused on design geared to necessity with an absence of unnecessary ornamentation. Gone were the romantic realism of the Victorian florals and the swirling Art Nouveau designs. Instead structure took precedence as shown in plates 2541, 2543, 2545, and 2557.

While we know that the Noritake company produced the greatest abundance of wares during the Nippon era (marks 47 and 52), it is unknown who produced the coralene pieces. However, some of the coralene vase and ewer molds appear to be the same as those used by the Noritake company. Therefore, it can be theorized that the Noritake company may have sold green ware blanks to those companies producing coralene. Further inspection of these blanks reveals that perhaps they were seconds as often the porcelain is not quite as fine as items bearing marks 47 or 52. At the present time, there are seven known coralene backstamps. Generally, the finer pieces bear the Kinran backstamp mark 244 although wonderful examples can be found bearing other backstamps. As you look through the coralene section, note the items with mark 244 and see if you agree. It is not known if "Kinran" was a manufacturer's name or if it had some other significance. If we assume that Kinran was a manufacturer and further assume that the "Royal Kinran" in marks 88 and 89 was the same company, I propose that we can theorize that Kinran devoted most of their energy into coralene production since few hand-painted Nippon pieces are found today with marks 88 and 89. Perhaps in the future we'll have more facts.

Virtually all items produced in Japan during the Nippon era utilize "Nippon" as the country of origin. Since "Nippon" is how the Japanese translate "Japan" into English and since the companies were undoubtedly Japanese owned, the use of "Nippon" makes sense. Why then was coralene marked with the word Japan? Could it be because an American held the patent on coralene production and, therefore, specified this word be used? Or could it mean that the companies producing the coralene were more directly influenced by Americans? Whatever the case, it is perhaps irrelevant. Obviously, coralene was produced during the Nippon era and is no less Nippon in spite of having the word "Japan" used as the country of origin.

As time progresses, perhaps we will learn even more about coralene. At the present time, however, we will have to be satisfied by the limited facts we have and the theories that are proposed. But, fortunately, this lack of knowledge does not hinder our appreciation and admiration of the many wonderful coralene items that have survived the ravages of time and have found their way into our collections. Take good care of them and handle them carefully so that the generations that follow us will be able to admire them as we do.

# Nippon Coralene

Nippon marked coralene pieces are unusual to find but do exist. The mark is a semicircle rising sun above the words RS NIPPON. Most Japanese coralene items, however, are stamped "Patented 2/9/1909 Japan 912171," others are marked "Patent Applied For No. 38257" with Japanese markings included, "Kinran Patent N. 16137 Japan," or the RS mark is often found backstamped on items with the word Japan instead of Nippon appearing.

There is a wide variety of pieces to be found, vases, ferners, lamps, ewers, teapots in an assortment of designs, florals, scenics, geometrics, even birds and dragons to mention a few. Most background have a matte finish.

Collectors should be careful to check the items for missing beads and it is advisable to not soak the pieces in water when cleaning as the beading may fall off.

A.L. Rock, an American living in Yokohama, Japan, was the first to perfect this technique and apply for a patent.

There has been a lot of confusion as to what constitutes coralene beading and how it was manufactured and in an attempt to clean up any misconceptions regarding these pieces a copy of the original patent has been secured and is included for reference.

A. L. ROCK.
POTTERY ORNAMENTATION.
APPLICATION FILED AUG. 19, 1908.

912,171. Patented Feb. 9, 1909.

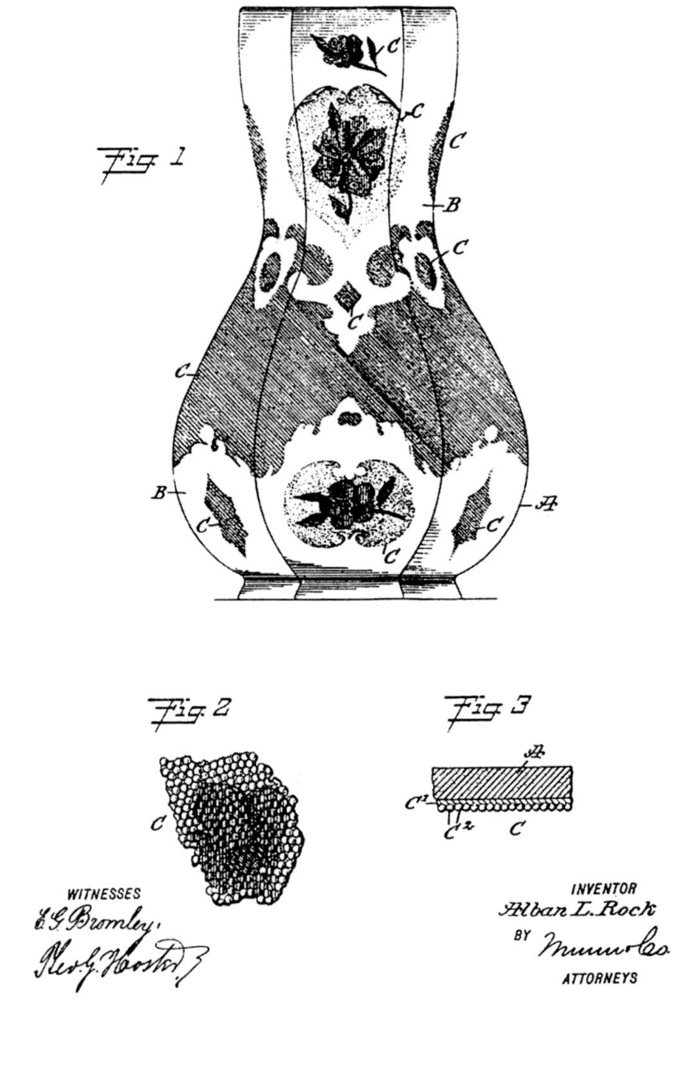

Fig 1

Fig 2

Fig 3

WITNESSES

INVENTOR
Alban L. Rock
BY Munn & Co.
ATTORNEYS

# UNITED STATES PATENT OFFICE.

ALBAN L. ROCK, OF YOKOHAMA, JAPAN, ASSIGNOR TO A. A. VANTINE & CO., OF NEW YORK, N. Y., A CORPORATION OF NEW JERSEY.

## POTTERY ORNAMENTATION.

**No. 912,171.** **Specification of Letters Patent.** **Patented Feb 9, 1909**

**Application filed August 19, 1908. Serial No. 449,223.**

*To all whom it may concern;*

Be it known, that I, ALBAN L. ROCK, a citizen of the United States, at present residing in Yokohama, Japan, have invented a new and Improved Pottery Ornamentation, of which the following is a full, clear, and exact description.

The object of the invention is to provide a new and improved pottery ornamentation, the ornamentation being arranged to produce a permanent glass bead effect on porcelain vases and other pottery articles, in such a manner that the colorless transparent glass beads are fused in position on the body of the pottery article by a fusing pigment which produces color effect in any predetermined design.

The invention consists of novel features and parts and combinations of the same, which will be more fully described herein-after and then pointed out in the claim.

A practical embodiment of the invention is represented in the accompanying drawings, forming a part of this specification, in which similar characters of reference indicate corresponding parts in all the views.

Figure 1 is a side elevation of a vase showing the improvement and produced according to my method; Fig. 2 is an enlarged side elevation of part of the same; and Fig. 3 is a transverse section of the same.

A portion of the surface of the body A of the base shown in Fig. 1, is ornamented by a suitable gold ornamentation B, and the remaining surface portion is covered by a glass bead ornamentation C, which consists of a fusing and carrying medium $C'$ and colorless transparent glass beads $C^2$ fused to the surface of the body A by the said fusing and carrying medium $C'$. The beads $C^2$ are comparatively small and are preferably spherical in shape, and the fusing and carrying medium $C'$ maybe in a plain uniform color or in many colors, according to predetermined design, as indicated at the portions representing the flowers on the vase shown in Fig. 1. The fusing and carrying medium $C'$ consists of porcelain pigments and a fusible matter, either mixed together prior to the application on the body, or applying the said pigments first and then the fusible matter. Sometimes both methods are used on the same article. As a rule, color work on porcelain showing bead decorations, is done in a dull color effect by means of mixing shiroye, balsam copaiba with oil of turpentine, and then the outline of the bead design is done by a specially prepared pigment which when fired results in the gold-moriage.

The principal components of the fusible matter are 248 grains of silicate of albumen (shiroye) and 192 grains of flux (hakukyoku) to which is added as a carrying medium about 9.6 grains of a dry procelain pigment or color, the several ingredients being mixed with a certain percentage of water and all parts are well ground together. The porcelain color or pigment used with the fusible matter to form the fusible and carrying medium $C'$ must be of such a shade as can be fired satisfactorily at a uniform degree of heat, as otherwise some of the colors will not be fired enough while other shades may be fired too much, and the slightest mistake in the selection of color shades in this respect tends to spoil the article.

In practice, the fusing and carrying medium $C'$ is applied to the body of the vase in a wet state, and then the colorless transparent glass beads $C^2$ are placed onto the said wet fusing and carrying medium, which holds the beads in position one alongside the other, as the rear portions of the beads are pressed into the wet medium. The vase or other article thus decorated is then fired in the usual manner, so that the beads are fused with their rear portions onto the porcelain body by the fusing and carrying medium, to permanently fix the beads in place without destroying their brilliant effect, enhanced by the underlying color pigment arranged accordingly to a predetermined design representing flowers and other objects.

It is understood that the colors of the fusing and carrying medium are refracted through the glass beads, thus giving the vase a very fine appearance in a plush effect.

It is understood that the selection of the fusible and carrying medium and the degree of heat used in firing is of importance as the fusible matter must necessarily fuse at a lower degree than the glass beads $C^2$, so that only the rear portions of the glass beads which are in contact with the fusible matter melt and fuse with the fusible matter, fused and adhering to the body A of the vase or like article.

It is important in the use of the glass bead covering for the predetermined pattern for the different particles to lie closely together and to be distributed thus uniformly in close contact with each other throughout the area of the pattern produced upon the vase or other article and this is accomplished by the form of beads and the fusing of said beads upon the pattern as distinguished from the production of a granulated surface which might vary both as to size and proximity of its particles. The glass granulated material is produced directly upon a pane of glass or the like. By the beaded construction it will be noticed that the surface ornamentation of the vase or other article will be approximately smooth and simulate a plain surface as to touch without affecting the beauty of appearance gained by the spherical form of the beads as shown.

Having thus described my invention, I claim as new and desire to secure by Letters Patent:

A vase or like pottery article having a body, a fusing and carrying medium disposed on said body and colored and shaped to conform to a predetermined design, and comparatively small colorless spherical transparent beads arranged in contact with each other and covering the carrying medium and fused into connection therewith and following the outline of the design produced by the fusing and carrying medium, whereby to form a covering for the medium which will be uniform throughout the extent of the design and through which the said medium will be refracted, giving to the article an ornamented appearance in plush effect.

In testimony whereof I have signed my name to this specification in the presence of two subscribing witnesses.

ALBAN L. ROCK.

Witness:
Genji Kuribara,
Masataro O. Kasava.

# Backstamps Found on Coralene Items

Mark #95
RS NIPPON
Found on coralene pieces.

Mark #241
RS JAPAN
Found on coralene pieces.

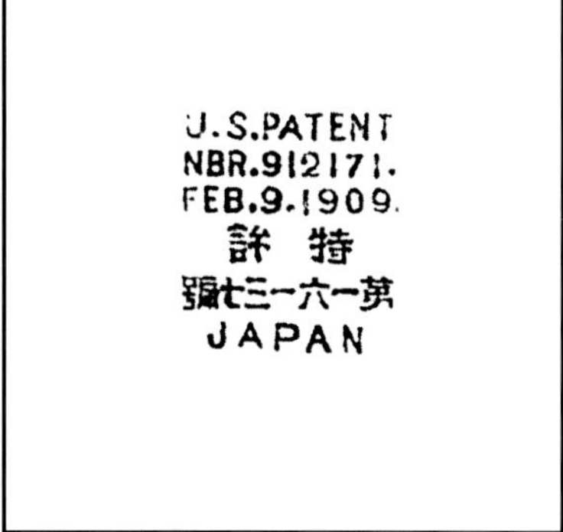


Mark #242
US Patent 912171
Found on coralene pieces. Top row translates "applied for," bottom row "16137."

Mark #243
US Patent 912171
Found on coralene pieces.

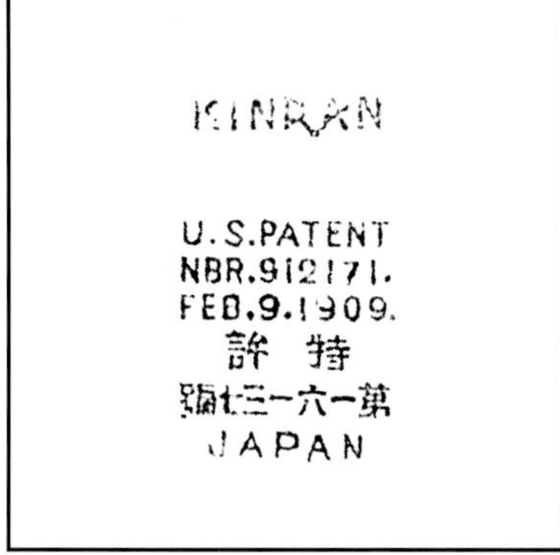


Mark #244
Kinran US Patent 912171
Found on coralene pieces.

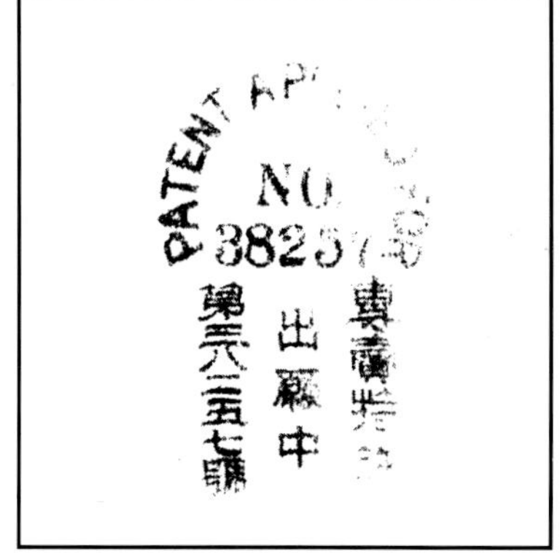


Mark #245
Patent applied for no. 38257
Found on coralene pieces.
Left vertical column translates "38257," center column "specialty sale," right column "Patent applied for."

Mark #246
Kinran patent no. 16187
Found on coralene pieces.

# Cobalt Blue

*by Judith Boyd*

Cobalt blue is the color of choice for many Nippon collectors. Cobalt blue can be found on every type of Nippon-marked item from relish dishes to bolted urns.

Within the cobalt blue field, there are many areas to choose from, if one wishes to further delineate a collection. For example, one may find pieces that are all cobalt with gold decoration, cobalt with scenes, cobalt with roses, cobalt with any other flower, prized pieces of cobalt with portraits, and even the rare cobalt blue and coralene pieces.

Cobalt blue may be used as a trim or border color on Nippon. Some pieces have scenes (or flowers) within various-shaped medallions and the cobalt is a background color over the rest (Figs. 9 & 10). There are also very desirable pieces that are all cobalt blue, overlaid with intricate gold designs and flowers.

Until 1869, the Japanese used "gosu" to obtain the cobalt color. Gosu is a pebble found in riverbeds. It had to be ground up and mixed with green tea before it could be applied to the porcelain. The tannin in the tea prevented the color from spreading where it didn't belong, when the glaze was applied.

In 1869, the Japanese began using imported cobalt oxide for the blue coloring. It was first used at the kilns in Narita. The imported cobalt oxide was more reliable than gosu and much easier to obtain. The color comes out strong and the application is even. This meant less possibility of streaking in the color.

Using the native gosu results in a soft, grayish-blue color, whereas using cobalt oxide results in the strong blue with which we are familiar. It does not take much imagination to assume that Japanese exporters preferred this eye-catching color to enhance their wares.

Most cobalt blue pieces are found with gold decoration. Some of it is quite elaborate. Even if the gold only consists of a little trim around the border, it is usually there. Because gold is expensive and cobalt oxide gives reliable results, it is understandable that these were used together. Hopefully, the aesthetics of the color combination were also considered.

Because cobalt blue is a rich color, suggesting the purple of royalty, pieces adorned with it usually have a formal appearance. For example, the cobalt and gold chocolate set would be used for company, not for the family every day (Fig 11).

Why are cobalt pieces so avidly collected? There is no accounting for the taste of collectors, but cobalt seems to have a special appeal to many Nippon-aholics. Cobalt is a rich and brilliant color that gives a substantial "air" to a piece. The regal color adds a certain elegance to any decoration. Nippon pieces decorated in cobalt blue do not hide on the shelf.

Figure 9.

Figure 10.

Figure 11.

# *Manning Bowman and Nippon*

*by Lee and Donna Call*

Some Nippon pieces were designed for metal holders of either polished copper or nickel plate. These exquisite designs were manufactured by Manning Bowman and Company and each style was individually numbered. All holders are engraved Manning Bowman Quality, Meriden, Connecticut, along with the catalog number.

Manning Bowman was founded in 1832 in Middletown, Connecticut, and the company moved to Meriden, Connecticut, in 1872. They specialized in manufacturing pots, pans, ladles, and funnels which were peddled throughout nearby towns by horse and wagon. The goods were hung on the outside of the wagon — the peddler slept inside. Their slogan was "MB means Best." The company developed mounted enamel ware, among them teapots and coffee pots decorated with flowers and handsome white metal mountings. Later, they were into percolators, chafing dishes, and copper tableware with English pewter mountings.

In 1912 they began making electric percolators, urn sets, electric sad irons, and bread toasters. For a number of years they designed and manufactured electric appliances for General Electric, Westinghouse, Sears, and the Jewel Tea Company. In 1938 they were bought out by Bersted Manufacturing Company and in 1946 they closed all operations in Meriden, Connecticut. Today Manning Bowman is a subsidiary of the MaGraw-Edison Company, more widely known for its Toast Master and now the company is called Toast Master Incorporated.

Several years ago we were lucky enough to obtain two old Manning Bowman catalogs. The following items shown are from catalog #65 and #70 which is dated August 15, 1917.

JVP note: To date all the Nippon china found with these metal wares has been backstamped with the magenta M in wreath mark. Some pieces have also been found with the initials MB in gold. The Nippon porcelain items found with these copper- and nickel-plated wares are referred to as imported hand-decorated china in the catalogs. It's easy to imagine that some of these holders have disappeared over the years and some of the pieces we now own may have originally been sold as a set from Manning Bowman.

Bonbon dish, 6½" x 4¼", Manning Bowman holder, nickel plated, mark #47 magenta.

Manning and Bowman holder, copper with wicker trim, 8½" high.

Manning Bowman bonbon dish, 6½" diameter, 5" tall, mark #47 magenta.

Coffee set, 14" diameter 10½" high (handle), copper cup holders and tray, M\B #2031, mark #47 magenta.

Nine piece demitasse set, nickel-plated cup holders, Manning Bowman, #47 magenta.

Pot, 7", cups, 2", mark #47 magenta.

Manning Bowman holders, nickel plated, 4¼" tall, 3½" diameter, mark #47 magenta.

Mayonnaise or Whipped Cream Bowl and Ladle.
Diameter of Bowl, 6 inches.

| | Nickel Plated. | Polished Copper. |
|---|---|---|
| No. 258. | $3.00 | $3.00 |

Bon Bon Dish.
No. 259. 6½ inch.
Nickel Plated. Polished Copper.

Bon Bon Dish.

| | Nickel Plated. | Polished Copper. |
|---|---|---|
| No. 260. 6½ inch. | $3.50 | $3.50 |

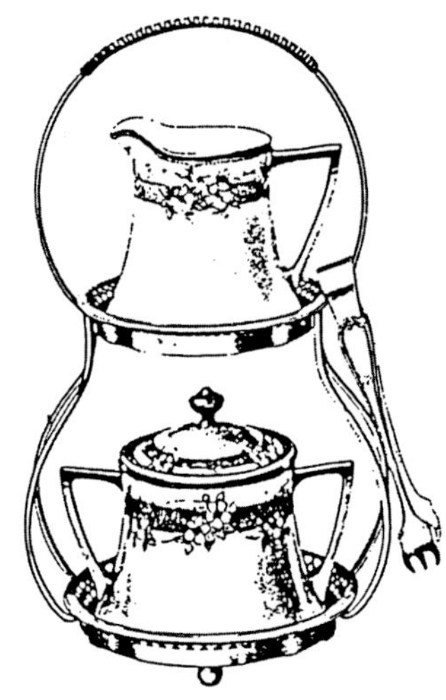

Dessert Set.

| | Nickel Plated. | Polished Copper. |
|---|---|---|
| No. 261. . . . | $4.50 | $4.50 |

Imported hand decorated sugar and cream.
Verona Tongs and holder with wicker handle.

| | | Nickel Plated. | Polished Copper. |
|---|---|---|---|
| No. 281. | Almond Bowl, 5½ inches, | $2.75 | $2.75 |
| 280. | Almond Dishes, set individual dishes, | 5.00 | 5.00 |

No. 2810. Almond Set, 7 Pieces. $7.75

Mayonnaise or Whipped Cream Bowl and Ladle.
Diameter of Bowl, 6 inches.

| | Nickel Plated. | Polished Copper. |
|---|---|---|
| No. 282. | $3.25 | $3.25 |

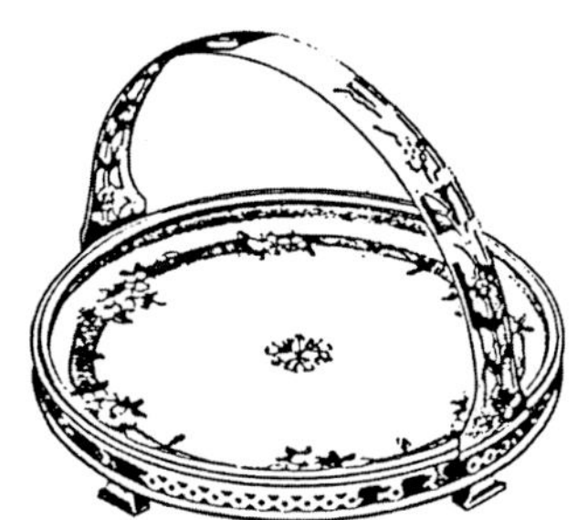

BON BON DISH.
No. 283. 6 inch.
Nickel Plated. Polished Copper.

FRUIT OR NUT BOWL.
Diameter, 7½ inches.

| | Nickel Plated. | Polished Copper. |
|---|---|---|
| No. 284. | $4.00 | $4.00 |

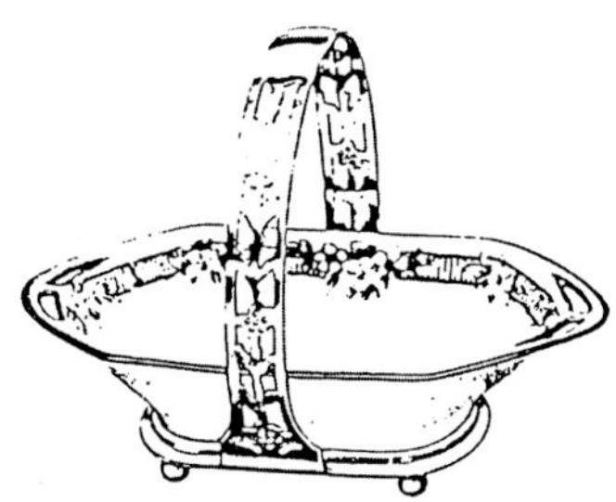

ALMOND DISH.
Size of dish, 4 x 7¼ inches.

| | Nickel Plated. | Polished Copper. |
|---|---|---|
| No. 286. | $3.00 | $3.00 |

No. 2860. ALMOND SET, 7 Pieces, . $8.00
Includes No. 286 Dish and set of 6 No. 280 Individual Almond Dishes as illustrated with No. 2810 set.

| | | Nickel Plated. | Polished Copper. |
|---|---|---|---|
| No. 285. | SALAD BOWL, 8½ inches, | $5.00 | $5.00 |
| 1068. | SPOON, | 2.50 | 2.50 |
| 1068. | FORK, | 2.50 | 2.50 |

The spoon and fork have mahogonite handles with saw pierced mountings. The bowls are heavily silver plated.

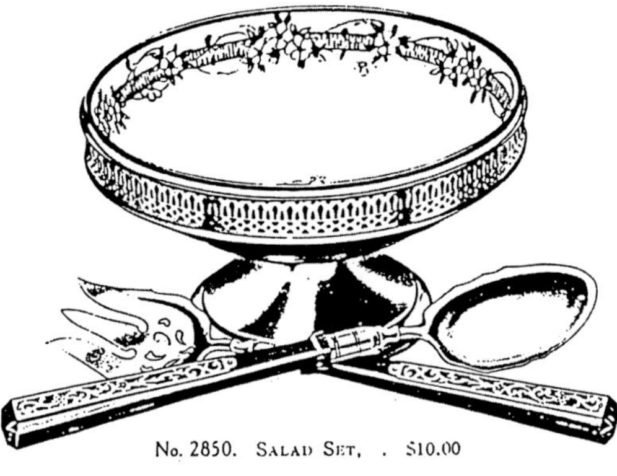

No. 2850. SALAD SET, . $10.00

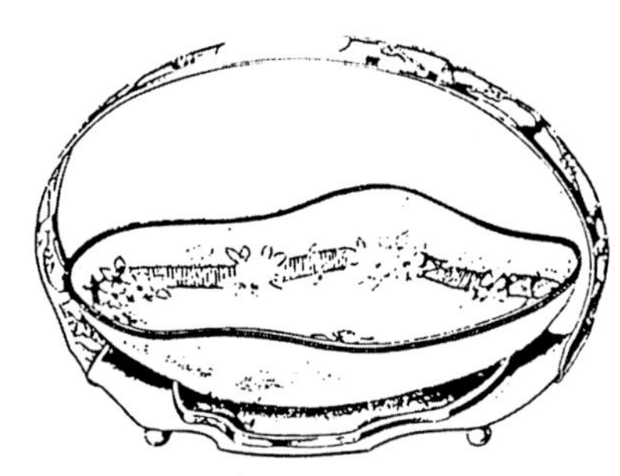

ALMOND DISH.
Size of dish, 4¼ x 7½ inches.

| | Nickel Plated. | Polished Copper. |
|---|---|---|
| No. 287. | $4.00 | $4.00 |

No. 2870. ALMOND SET, 7 Pieces, . $9.00
Includes No. 287 Dish and set of 6 No. 280 Individual Almond Dishes as illustrated with No. 2810 set.

## CHINA TEA BALL TEA POTS.

These have imported hand decorated china bodies, and are furnished both with nickel plated and silver plated mountings. They combine the exclusive advantages of our tea ball construction with the added superiority of a china body.

HAND DECORATED CHINA BODIES.
No. 972. 4 Cups, 1⅓ Pints.
973. 6 " 2¼ "

No. 2029. TEA SET, 4 Pieces.

| | |
|---|---|
| No. 972. | TEA BALL TEA POT, 4 cups. |
| 165. | SUGAR, Imported Hand Decorated China, 8 oz. |
| 165. | CREAM, " " " " 5 " |
| 2215. | TRAY, " " " " Lining. 11 x 7½ inches. |

The Tea Ball raised and locked under the cover.

The correct way to fill the Tea Ball.

Tea Ball filled with Tea and immersed in Boiling Water.

Tea now being made of the strength desired, the Tea Ball is raised and held under the cover by a novel locking device. By this process the second cup of tea, although it may remain much longer in the pot, retains the same delicious flavor as when first made.

No. 2025. Coffee Set, 10 Pieces.
No. 163. Coffee, Imported Hand Decorated China, 12 ounces.
163. Sugar, " " " " 6 "
163. Cream, " " " " 4 "
163. Cups and Metal Holders, Imported Hand Decorated China (set of 6).
9014. Tray, 14 inch (Wicker Handle).
Nickel Plated. Polished Copper.

No. 2027. Coffee Set, 10 Pieces.
No. 163. Coffee, Imported Hand Decorated China, 14 ounces.
163. Sugar, " " " " 6 "
163. Cream, " " " " 4 "
163. Cups and Metal Holders, Imported Hand Decorated China (set of 6).
9114. Tray, 14 inch (Hand Pierced Handle).
Nickel Plated. Polished Copper.

No. 2029. Tea Set, 4 pieces.
No. 972. Tea Ball Tea Pot, 4 cups.
165. Sugar, Imported Hand Decorated China, 8 ounce.
165. Cream, " " " " 5 "
2215. Tray, " " " " Lining, 11 x 7½ inches.
Tea Ball Tea Pot has Imported Hand Decorated China Body.
Nickel Plated. Polished Copper.

No. 2032. Coffee Set, 10 pieces.
No. 165. Coffee, Imported Hand Decorated China, 18 ounce.
165. Sugar, " " " " 8 "
165. Cream, " " " " 5 "
165. Cups and Metal Holders, Imported Hand Decorated China (set of 6).
2216. Tray, 14 inch with Removable Decorated China Center.
Nickel Plated. Polished Copper.

No. 2041. Coffee Set, 5 Pieces.
Nickel Plated. Polished Copper.
Oval Tray, 10 inch. Coffee Server, 5 ounce.
Cups, 2 ounce. Imported hand decorated china linings.
Sugar, 3 ounce.

No. 2201. Bouillon Cup, 6 ounces.
Diameter, 3¾ inches. Height, 2⅝ inches.
Nickel Plated. Polished Copper.

No. 2202. SHERBET CUP, 6 ounces.
Diameter, 3¾ inches. Height, 4⅜ inches.
Nickel Plated. Polished Copper.

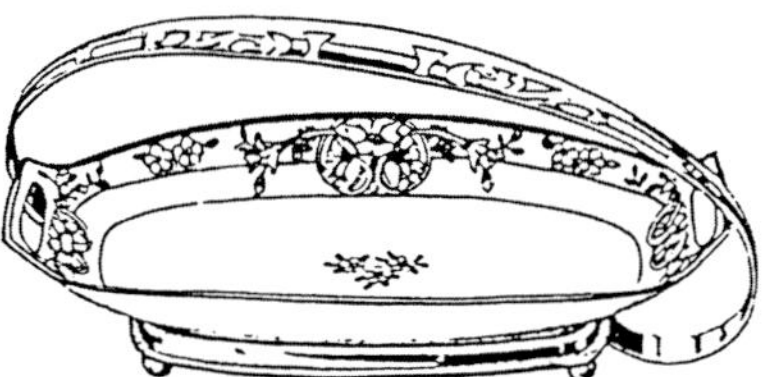

No. 2203. OLIVE DISH.
Size of dish, 4 x 8¼ inches.
Nickel Plated. Polished Copper.

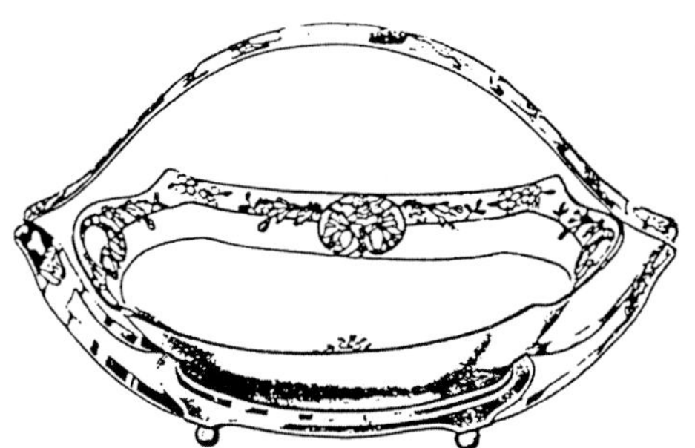

No. 2204. BON BON DISH.
Size of dish, 4¾ x 8 inches.
Nickel Plated. Polished Copper.

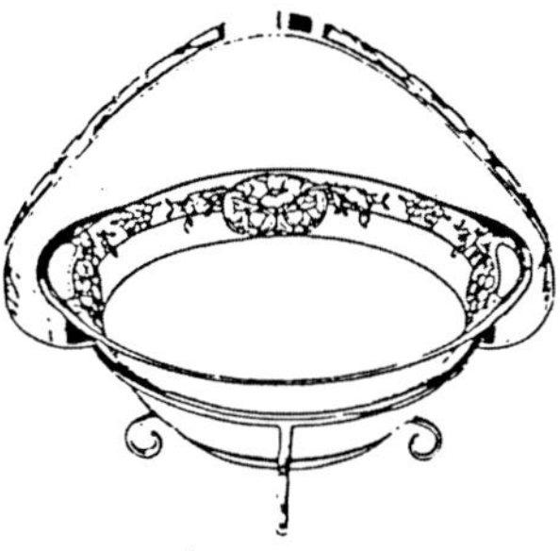

ALMOND DISH.
No. 2207. 5¾ x 6½ inches.
Nickel Plated. Polished Copper.

NUT BOWL.
No. 2208. 6¾ x 8 inches.
Nickel Plated. Polished Copper.

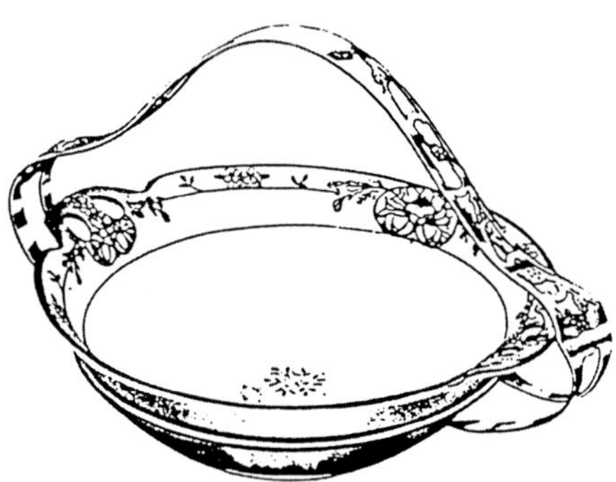

SALAD BOWL.
No. 2209. 9½ x 8 inches.
Nickel Plated. Polished Copper.

No. 2211. ALMOND SET.
Almond Bowl and six individual dishes.
Nickel Plated. Polished Copper.

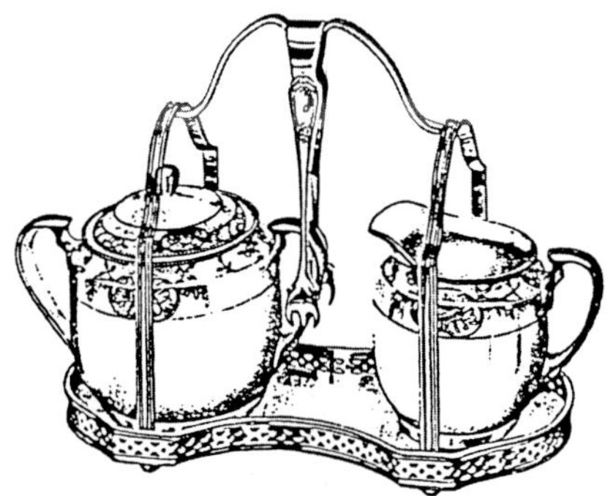

No. 2212. DESSERT SET.
Imported hand decorated china sugar and cream.
Silver Plated "Verona" Tongs.
Nickel Plated. Polished Copper.
Sugar, 8 ounce. Cream, 5 ounce.

No. 2213. Dessert Set.
Imported hand decorated china sugar and cream.
Nickel Plated. Polished Copper.
Sugar, 8 ounce. Cream, 5 ounce.

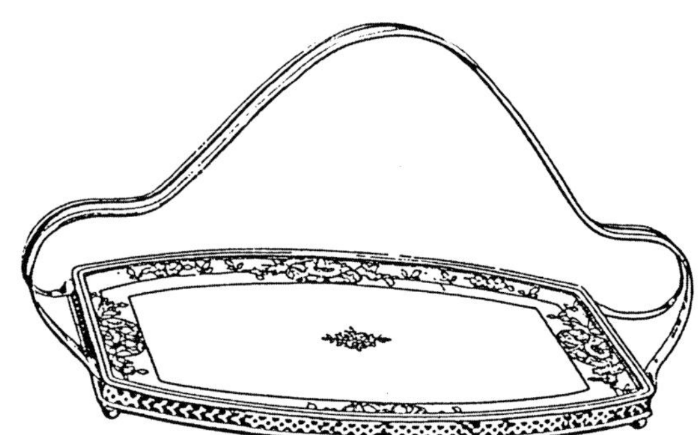

No. 2214. Serving Tray.
Imported Hand Decorated China Lining.
Size of china plate, 11 x 7½ inches.
Nickel Plated. Polished Copper.

Bon Bon Tray.
No. 2217. 7 inch.
Nickel Plated. Polished Copper.

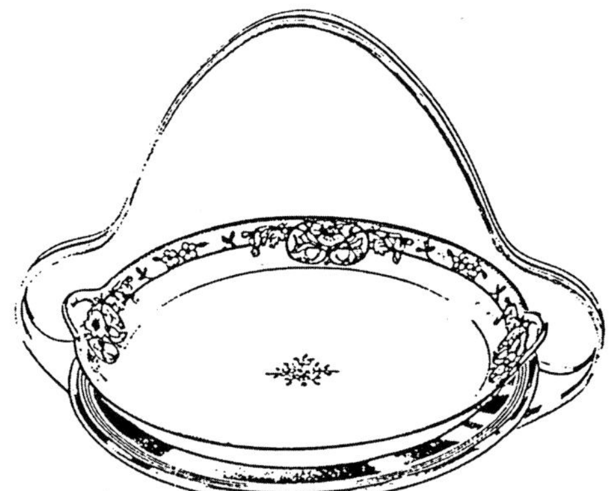

Cake Tray.
No. 2218. 9 inch.
Nickel Plated. Polished Copper.

Comport.
No. 2220. 6 inch.
Nickel Plated. Polished Copper.

Berry Bowl.
No. 2222. 7½ inch.
Nickel Plated. Polished Copper.

No. 2223. Berry Set, (2 pieces), Bowl, 7½ inch.
Nickel Plated. Polished Copper.

No. 2850. Salad Set.
No. 285. Salad Bowl, 8½ inch.
1068. Spoon.
1068. Fork.
Nickel Plated. Polished Copper.
Spoon and fork have Mahoganite handles with saw pierced mountings.

SALAD SET.

| | Nickel Plated. | Polished Copper. |
|---|---|---|
| No. 4037. | $8.00 | $8.00 |

Oil, Vinegar, Mayonnaise Bowl with Ladle, 2 Peppers and 1 Salt.
Mayonnaise Bowl and Ladle are imported hand decorated china.

No. 22020. SHERBET SET, 7 Pieces.
No. 2202. SHERBET DISHES, 6 ounces (set of 6).
Diameter, 3¾ inches. Height, 4⅜ inches.
No. 2221. TRAY, 14 inch.

No. 22010. BOUILLON SET, 7 pieces.
No. 2201. BOUILLON CUP, 6 ounces (set of 6).
Diameter, 3¾ inches. Height, 2⅝ inches.
No. 2221. TRAY, 14 inch.
Nickel Plated. Polished Copper.

No. 22100. SALAD SET.
No. 2210. SALAD BOWL, 8 x 9½ inches.
1064. SPOON, Mahoganite Handle.
1064. FORK, " "
Nickel Plated. Polished Copper.

No. 22220. BERRY SET, (4 pieces).
2220. " BOWL, 7½ inch.
163. SUGAR, 6 ounces.
163. CREAM, 4 "
6212. TRAY, 12 inch.
Nickel Plated. Polished Copper.

Berry Bowl and Tray may be used separately.

# *Nippon Urns*

*by Mark Griffin and Earl Smith*

Ahhh... those wonderful Nippon urns! In our opinion, there is nothing more representative of the beauty of Nippon than an urn... especially a palace urn. Although Webster's defines an urn as "a vessel that is typically an ornamental vase on a pedestal...," in the Nippon world, urns are generally referred to as any vase that is bolted, covered, or bolted and covered.

Nippon urns vary in size from as small as 8" to as large as 28" (or perhaps even larger — much is yet to be discovered!). While the most coveted urns are the palace urns measuring at least 24", there are many outstanding examples in the 16" to 22" range. Although size alone does not dictate one piece being more valuable than another of lesser size, generally the palace urns provide such magnificent examples of the artwork responsible for many of us falling in love with Nippon that they command the highest price. These palace urns are also the most scarce. Look closely at some of them and you will note the incredibly elaborate trim designs that must have taken a skilled artist considerable time to complete. The scenic panels, while often the same as found on other molds, have been masterfully adapted to fit the larger surface area upon which they have been hand painted. While none among us would declare them to reflect the same level of artistry of a Royal Vienna urn, these scenes and their execution evoke the warmth and passion for which Nippon is known. And, few of us, if any, would consider for even a moment trading a Nippon palace urn for a Royal Vienna palace urn! If you love Nippon as much as we do, you understand exactly what we mean.

Generally, most urns have the M in a wreath mark. The exceptions are portrait urns and some floral urns which have the maple leaf mark and coralene urns which have the patent mark. Since the M in a wreath mark is a later mark, these urns probably represent an evolution in the marketing efforts of the Noritake company during the Nippon era. Evidently, the Japanese felt they could successfully compete against the European manufacturers and started producing these larger urns as a result. The time and expense to produce these must have been considerable even by turn-of-the-century standards. Thus, today they are very scarce and highly valued.

While we do not know for certain all the avenues through which the finer Nippon items were sold, we can be certain that they were not Larkin premiums. It is thought that the better Nippon items were sold in the better department, jewelry, and gift stores of the time. While perhaps priced less than the European porcelains they were competing against for the consumer's dollar, the fine Nippon items we all have in our collections today must have been treasured by the purchaser as evidenced by their survival through the decades. Many pieces are in such perfect condition that they appear to have had a special spot in a china cabinet and have passed through the generations as a much-treasured family heirloom.

These wonderful urns are but a small part of the world of Nippon. The vast diversity of quality Nippon items is what makes collecting Nippon so exciting! Whether your preference is urns, blownouts, plaques, portraits, hatpin holders, moriage, coralene, ashtrays, humidors, dolls, tea sets, or chocolate sets, you'll find quality Nippon items to satisfy your desire.

Bolted urn, 16" tall, backstamped, green mark #47.

Bolted covered urn, 19" tall, backstamped, green mark #47.

# *Care and Cleaning of Nippon*

***by Earl Smith***

What is the proper way to clean your Nippon porcelain? First, you must ready your supplies. You'll need the following to thoroughly and safely clean your Nippon:

- Cotton dish towels
- A plastic dishpan
- Ivory® liquid dish detergent
- Formula 409® cleaner
- A well-worn soft bristle toothbrush
- Bottle brush — cloth or foam
- Toothpicks
- Cotton swabs
- Comet® cleanser
- Goo-Gone® cleaner
- Non-oily fingernail polish remover
- Gum eraser
- Rolled cotton

And lots of patience

First, remove as much as possible from your kitchen countertops so you will have an unobstructed work surface. Place the plastic dishpan in the sink and fill ⅓ with warm, sudsy water. The plastic dishpan will provide a softer surface than a porcelain or stainless steel sink, thus reducing the risk of damage. The sudsy water will provide you with the moisture you'll need to dip the toothbrush in as you proceed with the cleaning.

Next, before wetting the item to be cleaned, remove unwanted labels and label residue with Goo-Gone. Other foreign matter such as paint splatters may be removed by carefully using a cotton swab dipped in fingernail polish remover. (It's amazing how many pieces I've had that had small paint drops on them — especially wall plaques!)

Now, generously spray the entire piece with Formula 409. I enjoy seeing all the dirt come off, so I spray in the other sink bowl lined with a white cotton dish towel (it's the little things in life, you know!). After thoroughly spraying with Formula 409, place the item in the dishpan (or hold it over the pan, depending on the mold) and gently scrub the piece with the well-worn toothbrush. Be extra-gentle when cleaning moriage or coralene so as not to dislodge any by applying too much pressure. If necessary, rinse occasionally to see if extra cleaning is required. (Make sure the faucet is totally out of the way during cleaning.) Clean the inside of vases, etc. with the bottle brush. Keep focused on what you are doing and make sure you always have a firm grip on the item you are cleaning. Avoid holding by handles as they are a weak point.

With the general cleaning finished, thoroughly rinse the entire piece with warm water. Fill the inside of vases, until all suds are gone and water runs clear. As a side note, you want to have a plastic faucet head and a removable spray attachment so you don't have to move the piece around the water flow. You want to be able to move the water flow around the piece. A fixed metal faucet may result in damage by hitting against the item. And, besides, the sound of porcelain breaking is one not for the weak of heart! Place your cleaned piece on a cotton dish towel to catch water runoff (although more absorbent, bath towels are too thick and may not provide a stable work surface). Examine well to see if extra cleaning is required. Occasionally, a stubborn spot can be removed by dabbing your fingertip or the toothbrush in Comet and rubbing gently. Other foreign debris may require the use of a toothpick to dislodge especially if it is within moriage decoration. More stubborn marks on bisque finishes may require an eraser to remove. If an eraser is used, use only a gum eraser, not the pink ones on the end of a pencil. Wait until the piece is completely dry before attempting to use the eraser.

Now, pat the piece dry with a soft absorbent cotton dish towel and allow it to air dry while you record your purchase.

Most important of all: Do not become distracted! Keep focused on what you are doing to reduce the risk of an accident. This applies, also, when you place the piece in its new home. Don't take chances. If needed, move another piece before placing your new piece next to it. It's well worth the extra time.

The final step is used only on gold or gloss finishes. Gently buff these surfaces with a piece of rolled cotton. I don't know why for sure, but this brings out the lustre of these finishes significantly. I assume it must remove small amounts of residue left behind. As always, be gentle.

These cleaning methods may be used on all types of Nippon, as I have never had a problem with using any of these cleaning materials or techniques. Some do not suggest cleaning moriage or coralene as described above; but, I have found that a good dousing with Formula 409 and gentle scrubbing removes the grime between the moriage beading, slipwork, and glass beads. Just use common sense in deciding how hard to scrub with the toothbrush. A very gentle brushing is usually all that's needed.

I hope this information helps those of you who may be concerned about cleaning your Nippon. Many pieces are almost a hundred years old and take on new life when they're cleaned up. You'll be surprised how much more beautiful they are when you remove those decades of grime.

Happy Cleaning!

WARNING: if an item has been restored, clean with extreme caution. Cleaning will remove certain types of restoration.

# Nippon Reproductions

Today, so-called Nippon reproductions are flooding the antique and collectible market. The minute something becomes popular it rises in price and someone sets out to reproduce it. A reproduction is intended to take the place of the antique without deceit but the new fakes are a direct attempt to deceive the public. These are not really reproductions but an attempt to place a so-called Nippon backstamp on new porcelain.

Many of the pieces are not bad for the wholesale price but remember that ten years from now the repro will only be a secondhand item and the Nippon piece if carefully chosen should increase in value. When we buy Nippon era wares we're paying for age and quality and with the repro, neither is there.

Just because an item is sold at an antique shop or show or at an auction or an estate sale where most of the items appear to be old this does not mean that genuine pieces of Nippon will be found there. These new items have been designed to deceive!

Presently, the pieces I am aware of are being imported to wholesalers in the United States from both Japan and China. Wholesale prices run anywhere from $4 – $6.50 for hatpin holders, candlesticks cost $15, vases are $13 – 40, tea sets can be as high as $95 with six cups and saucers, shaving mugs run around $10, and tankards are about $70. All types of items are being sold, chocolate sets, cookie jars, perfume bottles, trinket boxes, bells, urns, vases, butter dishes, the list goes on and on.

Our present customs rules allow these items into the country and I see no end in sight. When I wrote Series III I only knew of eight patterns and now there are over 30 and probably many more to come.

The McKinley Tariff Act was passed in 1890 and stated that as of March 1, 1891, all articles of foreign manufacture shall be marked in legible English words so as to indicate the country of their origin. This was to be done as nearly indelible and permanent as the nature of the article would permit.

On February 8, 1917, our Treasury Dept. decided that chinaware and porcelain not marked to indicate the country of origin at the time of importation may be released when marked by means of a gummed label or with a rubber stamp.

The Treasury Dept. further ruled that as of October 1, 1921, that Nippon was a Japanese word the English equivalent of which was Japan and from that date on all items now had to be marked Japan.

Since Nippon is not considered the name of a country in English words at the present time, the fake backstamps under the glaze are allowed when a paper label is affixed indicating the actual country of origin. If the item is made in China and has a label attesting to this fact then the item is allowed into the United States. The mark under the glaze has no bearing with the importation ruling.

After purchase, the paper label is easily removed and magically we now have a Nippon marked item.

So far, I have found nine fake backstamps. There are three in a wreath. The M in wreath which is missing the stem on the three leaf figure, the K in an upside down wreath, and the hourglass also in an upside down wreath. There are two rising suns; the one from Japan has the rays zigzagged, the Chinese one has fewer rays and the sun part is not solid in color as the real one is. The fake RC mark is all in green whereas the genuine one has the words "hand painted" in red. The fake maple leaf mark is about ½" in size and the genuine one is only about ¼". The fake spoke or komaru mark has the words "hand painted" in a curve and the real one has these words in a straight line. And then we are finding the word Nippon stamped on the figural alligator piece. The boy on the alligator can also be found bearing an Occupied Japan mark and some of the other fake Nippon pieces come with a Limoges or R.S. Prussia backstamp.

Collectors and dealers must keep informed regarding these wares. Check the INCC newsletters, antique trade papers and magazines, Nippon reference books, and share your information with others. If possible, handle and feel the repros. Many are easily spotted but some take more time and can present a problem until collectors learn their way around. The glazing is different and on some of the Chinese pieces the inside of the vases are not even glazed.

The use of colors is different, the weight is not the same, the gold trim is usually of a luster type, and there is seldom any lack of wear. Some may even be similar in shape to the genuine pieces.

When you are out shopping, one tip-off is when you find items at antique shops and shows far below the market price.

Beware. It's possible, but this may be a clue that the item is not genuine. Or, you suddenly see a number of items in the same pattern in any one shop, booth, or auction. Be extra careful when you start seeing the exact same item time after time when you are out shopping. Another clue is when you see an uncommon piece in the same shape and pattern in a number of shops. Get to know your Nippon, both genuine and fake. Buy from reputable dealers and ask for a written guarantee. If in doubt, don't buy.

Genuine piece on left. Fake on right.

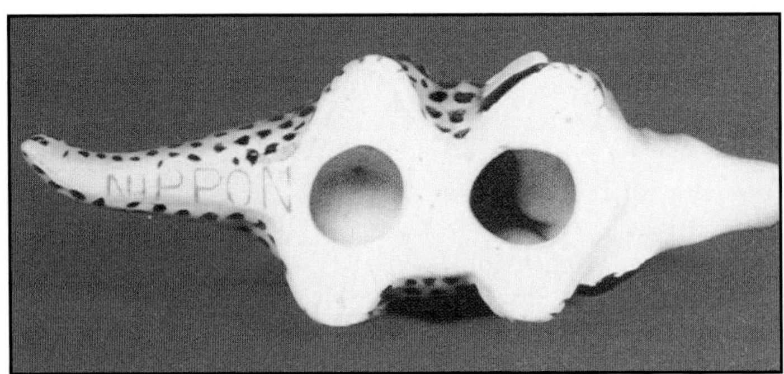

| Genuine Backstamps | Fake Backstamps | | |
|---|---|---|---|
|  Original M in wreath mark. |  No stem. | 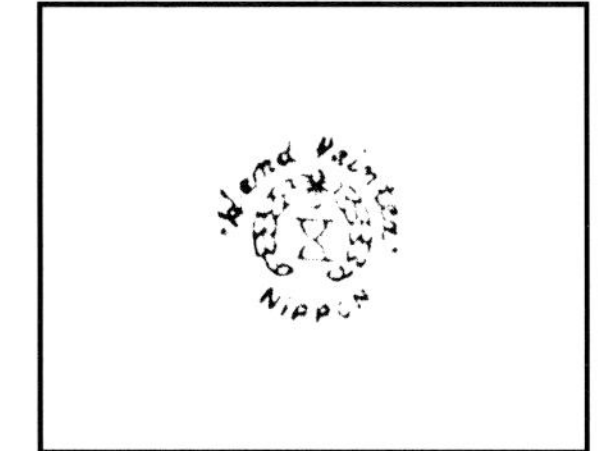 Upside down wreath. |  Upside down wreath. |
|  Genuine rising sun mark. |  Japanese mark. |  Chinese mark. | |
|  Genuine maple leaf mark. Original ¼" leaf. | 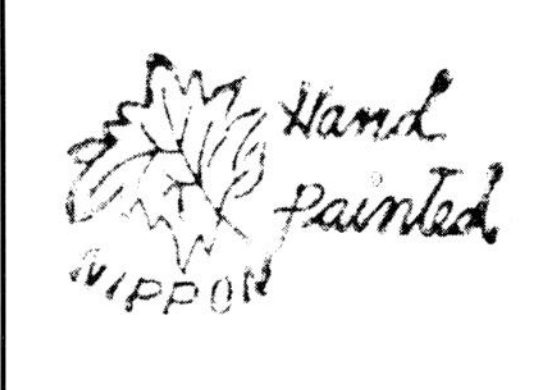 Fake ½" leaf. | | |
|  Genuine RC mark. |  Fake RC mark. | The words "hand painted" on original mark are in red, the rest is in green. Fake mark is all green. | |
|  Genuine komaru mark. |  Fake komaru mark. | On the genuine spoke or komaru, "hand painted" is straight across. | |
| NIPPON | Stamped on – shown on alligator's tail. | | |

Green Mist Pattern:
sugar bowl and creamer, powder box, master sugar bowl, crimped sugar bowl, tea set.

Pink Luster Pattern:
hatpin holder, four chocolate sets.

Wildflower Pattern:
four chocolate or mocha sets, urn, dresser jar, egg box, tea strainer, candlestick, lemonade set, footed box, hinged powder box, trinket box, ewer, butter dish, letter valet, bell, two dresser sets, sauce tureen, berry set, shaving mug, slanted cheese, shell dish, chamberstick, sugar bowl and creamer, bathroom set, oval box, powder dish.

Antique Spring Song Pattern: tankard or pitcher.

Antique Bouquet Pattern: tankard or pitcher.

Antique Rose Pattern:
creamer and sugar bowl, two sizes of cream pitchers, night set, salt and pepper, flask vase, tankard, mug, basket vase, tea set, tankard or pitcher, coffee set.

Antique Red Rose Pattern:
tankard or pitcher, two vases.

Texas Rose Pattern:
night set, ewer, cream pitcher, cup and saucer, tea set.

Other Texas Rose Pattern:
ewer.

Dogwood Pattern:
five chocolate or mocha sets, dresser set, oval box, footed bowl, heart box, berry set, trinket box, tea warmer, biscuit jar.

American Beauty Pattern:
coffee set.

Pink Mist Pattern:
tea set.

Pattern name unknown, has blue colored tint: shaving mug.

Chantilly Rose Pattern:
four tea sets, shaving mug, three hatpin holders.

Beige Chantilly Pattern:
three hatpin holders, shaving mug.

Wall plaque.

Pattern name unknown:
two vases, one 10" tall, one 14" tall with doll handles; 6" hatpin holder; 10" candlestick.

Pattern name unknown:
6" hatpin holder, jardiniere, 2¾" diameter, 8" vase, 18" umbrella stand.

Pattern name unknown:
4" tall hatpin holder, egg.

Pattern name unknown:
vase, 4" tall hatpin holder, egg.

Pattern name unknown:
two vases, 6" hatpin holder.

Pattern name unknown:
14" vase.

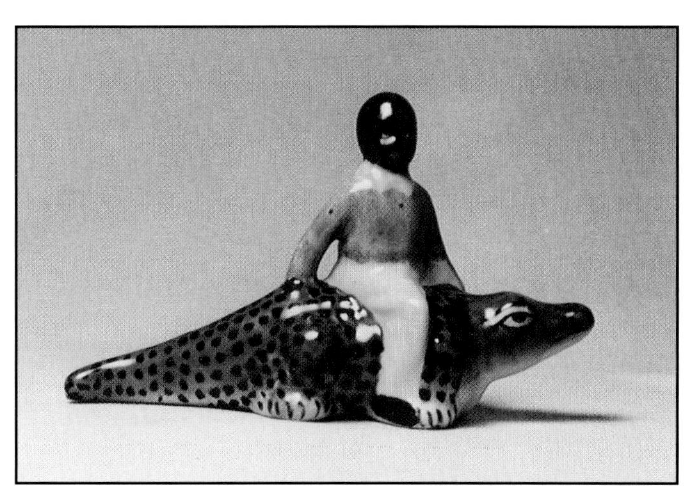

Figural black boy on alligator.

Pattern name unknown:
7½" vase.

Pattern name unkown:
bowl, 4" diameter; 4" tall hat-pin holder.

Pattern name unknown:
10" candlestick.

Pattern name unknown:
two 12" vases, 10" vase, 4" hatpin holder.

Rear view showing design featured
on both 10" and 12" vase.

Pattern name unknown:
10" vase.

Pattern name unknown:
8" vase.

# *Pricing*

Today's collectible market is constantly changing, what's in favor today may not be tomorrow. The values listed in this book are an estimated retail price for similar items in mint condition. Adjustments should be made for cracks, chips, worn gold, repairs, etc. The prices shown should be used only as a guide and are not intended to set prices which vary from one section of the country to another and from collector to collector.

When determining the value of an item one must take into account the condition of the piece, its rarity, quality of workmanship, aesthetic appeal, and popularity. Beautiful and well-executed pieces continue to spiral. Plainer, utilitarian type items rise little in value. Collecting fads will temporarily push the market up for a particular type or style but eventually prices do adjust back down. The demand for the wonderful rare items continues and since the demand far exceeds the supply these prices continue to go up and up.

Several people have contributed their time and expertise to make this a viable and realistic guide. Recent auctions, shows, and known sale prices were also taken into account. Prices shown should be considered as a starting point in determining a value. At their best most will be controversial, too high for some, too low for others. My advice is don't buy just for investment. Buy quality pieces you like at a price that seems fair.

# *Facsimiles & Photos of Marks Found on Nippon Items*

BABY BUD
NIPPON

1. Baby Bud Nippon; incised on doll.

BARA
HAND PAINTED
NIPPON

2. Bara hand painted Nippon.

3. The Carpathia M Nippon.

4. Cherry blossom hand painted Nippon; found in blue, green, and magenta colors.

5. Cherry blossom in a circle hand painted Nippon.

6. Chikusa hand painted Nippon.

7. China E-OH hand painted Nippon; found in blue and green colors.

8. Crown (pointed), hand painted Nippon; found in green and blue colors.

9. Crown Nippon (pointed) Made in Nippon; found in green and blue colors.

10. Crown (square), hand painted Nippon; found in green and green with red colors.

11. Chubby LW & Co. Nippon; found on dolls.

15. Double T Diamond in circle Nippon.

12. D Nippon.

16. Dowsie Nippon.

13. Dolly sticker found on Nippon's Dolly dolls, sold by Morimura Bros.

17. EE Nippon.

14. Double T Diamond, Nippon.

18. Elite B hand painted Nippon.

19. FY 401 Nippon; found on dolls.

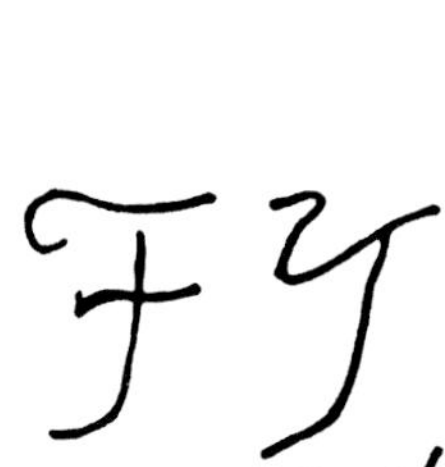


20. FY 405 Nippon; found on dolls.

21. G in a circle hand painted Nippon.

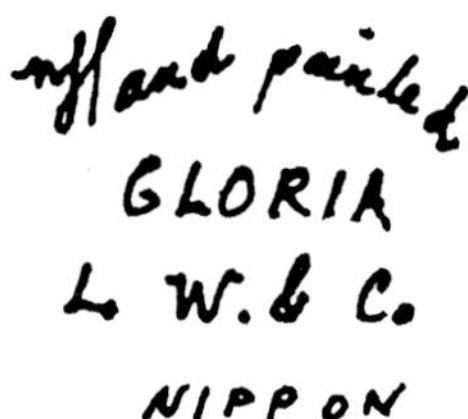


22. Gloria L.W. & Co. hand painted Nippon (Louis Wolf Co., Boston, Mass. & N.Y.C.).

23.Hand painted Nippon.

24. Hand painted Nippon.

25. Hand painted Nippon.

26. Hand painted Nippon.

27. Hand painted Nippon.

28. Hand painted Nippon with symbol.

29. Hand painted Nippon with symbol.

30. Hand painted Nippon with symbol.

31. Hand painted Nippon with symbol.

32. Hand painted Nippon with symbol.

33. Hand painted Nippon with symbol.

34. Hand painted Nippon with symbol.

35. Hand painted Nippon with symbol.

36. Horsman No. 1 Nippon; found on dolls.

37. IC Nippon.

38. Imperial Nippon; found in blue and green.

39. JMDS Nippon.

40. Jonroth Studio hand painted Nippon.

41. Kid Doll M.W. & Co. Nippon.

42. Kinjo Nippon.

43. Kinjo China hand painted Nippon.

L & CO

NIPPON

44. L & Co. Nippon.

45. LFH hand painted Nippon.

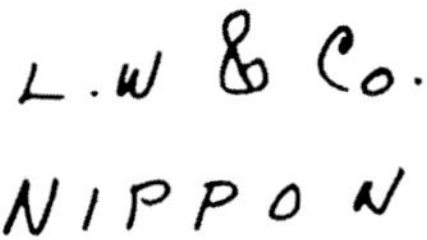


46. LW & Co. Nippon (Louis Wolf & Co., Boston, Mass & N.Y.C.).

50. M M hand painted Nippon.

47. M in wreath, hand painted Nippon (M stands for importer, Morimura Bros.); found in green, blue, magenta & gold colors. Mark used since 1911.

51. Made in Nippon.

48. M in wreath hand painted Nippon, D.M. Read Co. (M stands for importer, Morimura Bros.).

52. Maple leaf Nippon; found in green, blue, and magenta, dates back to 1891.

49. M B (Morimura Bros.) Baby Darling sticker; found on dolls.

53. Morimura Bros. sticker found on Nippon items.

54. Mt. Fujiyama Nippon.

NIPPON

55. Nippon found in blue, gold, and also incised into items.

NIPPON 84

56. Nippon 84.

NIPPON 144

57. Nippon 144.

221
NIPPON

58. Nippon 221.

59. Nippon with symbol.

60. Nippon with symbol.

61. Nippon with symbol.

NIPPON

62. Nippon with symbol.

63. Nippon with symbol.

64. Nippon with symbol.

ИIPPOИ

65. Nippon M incised on doll (note N is written backwards); #12 denotes size of doll; M = Morimura Bros.

66. Noritake M in wreath Nippon; M = Morimura Bros., found in green, blue, and magenta.

67. Noritake Nippon found in green, blue, and magenta colors.

68. Noritake Nippon found in green, blue & magenta colors. Mark used as early as 1906.

69. OAC Hand painted Nippon (Okura Art China, branch of Noritake Co.).

70. Oriental china Nippon.

71. Pagoda hand painted Nippon.

72. Patent #30441 Nippon.

73. Paulownia flowers & leaves hand painted Nippon (crest used by Empress of Japan, kiri no mon); found in a green/red color.

74. Paulownia flowers & leaves hand painted Nippon (crest used by Empress of Japan, kiri no mon).

75. Pickard etched china, Noritake Nippon; Pickard mark is in black; Noritake/Nippon mark is blue in color.

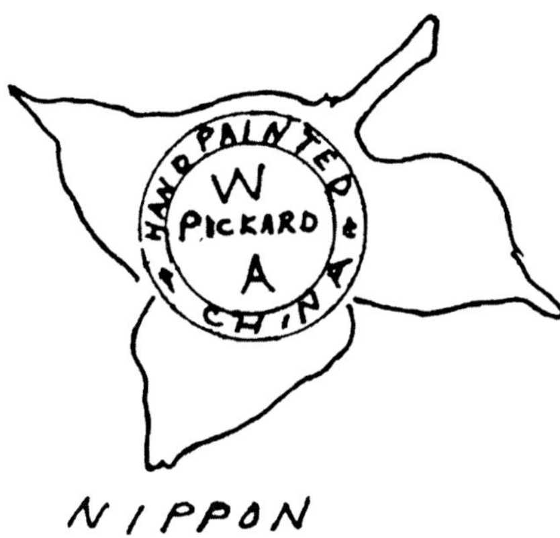


76. Pickard hand painted china Nippon.

77. Pickard hand painted china, Noritake Nippon; Pickard mark printed in black Noritake; Nippon in magenta.

78. Queue San Baby Sticker; found on Nippon dolls.

79. RC Nippon; RC stands for Royal Crockery (fine china).

80. RC hand painted Nippon combination of both red & green colors. RC stands for Royal Crockery (fine china). Mark used since 1911.

81. RC Noritake Nippon hand painted found in green & blue. RC stands for Royal Crockery (fine china). This mark has been in existence since 1906.

82. RC Noritake Nippon made for domestic market in Japan since 1902. RC stands for Royal Crockery (fine china).

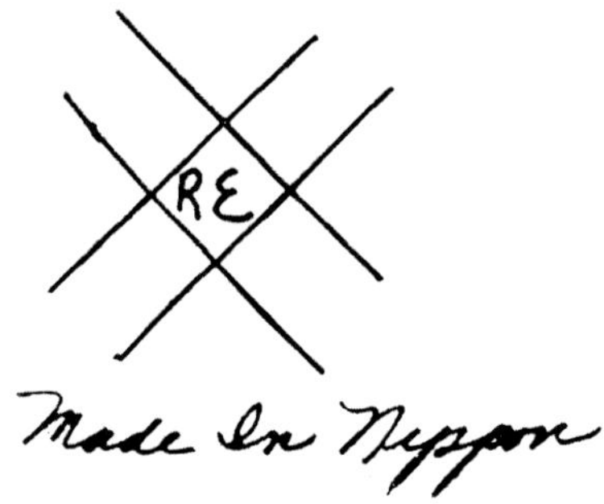


83. RE Nippon.

87. Royal Kaga Nippon.

84. Rising Sun Nippon.

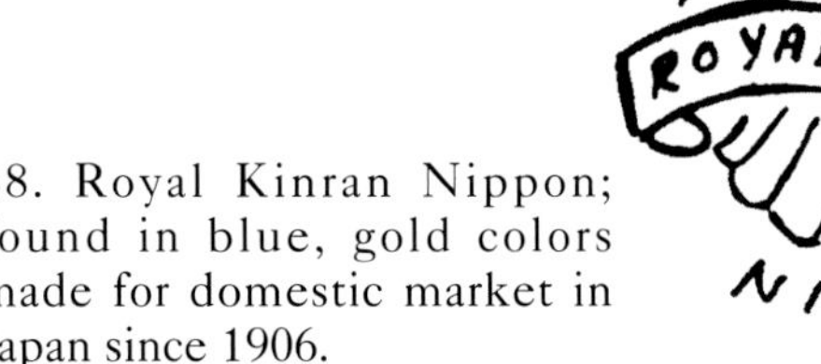

88. Royal Kinran Nippon; found in blue, gold colors made for domestic market in Japan since 1906.

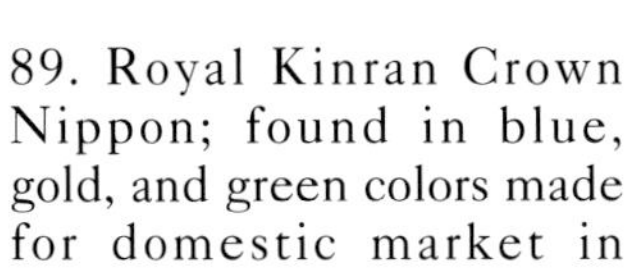

89. Royal Kinran Crown Nippon; found in blue, gold, and green colors made for domestic market in Japan since 1906.

Royal Dragon mark:


85. Royal Dragon Nippon.

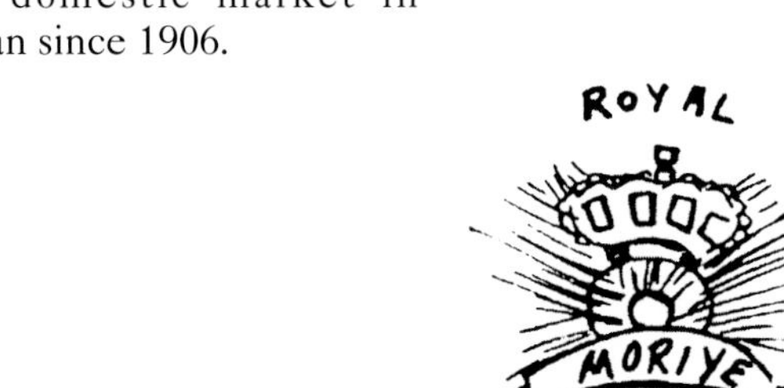


90. Royal Moriye Nippon; found in green and blue colors.

86. Royal Dragon Nippon Studio hand painted.

91. Royal Nishiki Nippon; made for domestic market in Japan since 1906.

92. Royal Satsuma Nippon (cross within a ring, crest of House of Satsuma); made for domestic market in Japan since 1906.

93. Royal Sometuke Nippon; made for domestic market in Japan since 1906.

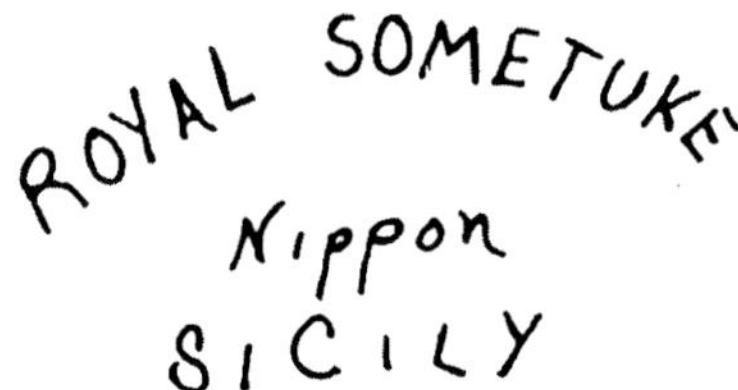


94. Royal Sometuke Nippon Sicily.

95. RS Nippon; found on coralene pieces.

96. S & K hand painted Nippon; found in green, blue, and magenta colors.

97. S & K hand painted Nippon; found in green, blue, and magenta colors.

98. Shinzo Nippon.

99. Shofu Nagoya Nippon.

100. SNB Nippon.

101. SNB Nagoya Nippon.

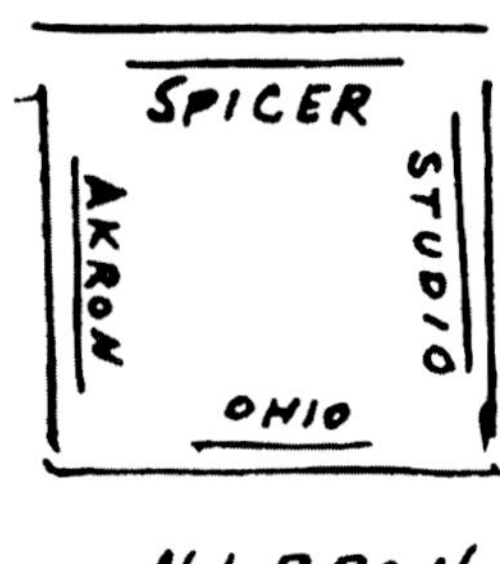


102. Spicer Studio Akron Ohio Nippon.

103. Spoke hand painted Nippon; mark in existence as early as 1906.

104. Studio hand painted Nippon.

105. Superior hand painted Nippon.

106. T Nippon (2 ho-o birds).

107. T hand painted Nippon.

108. T in wreath hand painted Nippon.

109. T N hand painted Nippon; mark is red and green.

110. TS hand painted Nippon.

111. TS hand painted Nippon.

112. Teacup Nippon.

113. Torii Nippon.

114. Tree crest Nippon (crest of Morimura family).

115. Tree Crest & Maple leaf hand painted Nippon.

117. Yamato hand painted Nippon.

116. V Nippon, Scranton, PA.

118. Yamato Nippon.

119. C.G.N. hand painted Nippon; found in green.

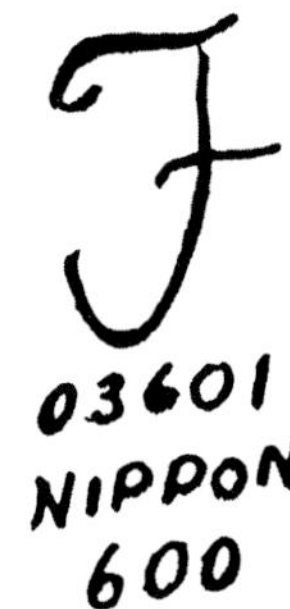


120. F Nippon 03601 600; found incised on dolls.

121. F. Nippon #76012 601; found incised on dolls.

122. F. Nippon #76018 30/3; found incised on dolls.

123. F. Nippon #76018 403.

124. FY Nippon; found incised on dolls.

125. FY Nippon 301; found incised on dolls.

126. FY Nippon 402; found incised on dolls.

127. FY 9 Nippon 402; found incised on dolls.

128. FY Nippon 404; found incised on dolls.

129. FY Nippon 406; found incised on dolls.

130. FY Nippon 464; found incised on dolls.

131. FY Nippon #17604 604; found incised on dolls.

132. FY Nippon #70018 004; found incised on dolls.

133. FY Nippon (variation of mark) #70018 403; found incised on dolls.

134. FY Nippon #70018 406; found incised on dolls.

135. FY Nippon (variation of mark) #70018 406; found incised on dolls.

136. FY Nippon #76018; found incised on dolls.

137. Jollikid sticker (red & white); found on dolls.

138. Ladykin sticker (red & gold); found on dolls.

NIPPON

139. Nippon (notice reversal of first N); found incised on items.

NIPPON
D13495

140. Nippon D13495; found in green.

NIPPON
E

141. Nippon E; found incised on dolls.

O
NIPPON

142. Nippon O; found incised on dolls.

5
NIPPON

143. Nippon 5; found incised on dolls.

97
NIPPON

144. Nippon 97; found incised on dolls.

98
NIPPON

145. Nippon 98; found incised on dolls.

99
NIPPON

146. Nippon 99; found incised on dolls.

101
NIPPON

147. Nippon 101; found incised on dolls.

102
NIPPON

148. Nippon 102; found incised on dolls.

105
NIPPON

149. Nippon 105; found incised on dolls.

123
NIPPON

150. Nippon 123; found incised on dolls.

151. Nippon 144 with symbol; found incised on dolls.

152. RE Nippon.

153. RE made in Nippon; found incised on dolls.

154. RE Nippon A9; found incised on dolls.

155. RE Nippon B8; found incised on dolls.

156. RE Nippon O 2; found incised on dolls.

157. Royal Hinode Nippon; found in blue.

158. Sonny sticker (gold, red, white & blue); found on dolls.

159. Maruta Royal Blue Nippon.

160. Hand Painted Coronation Ware Nippon.

161. ATA Imperial Nippon.

162. Baby Doll, M.W. & Co. Nippon sticker; found on dolls.

163. BE, 4 Nippon.

164. Cherry blossom Nippon, similar to No. 4.

165. Cherry blossom (double) Nippon.

166. C O L Nippon.

167. C.O.N. Hand Painted Nippon.

168. FY Nippon 405.

169. FY Nippon 505.

170. FY Nippon 601.

171. FY Nippon 602.

172. FY Nippon 1602.

173. FY Nippon 603 NO. 76018.

174. Happifat Nippon sticker; found on dolls.

175. H in circle Nippon.

176. Horsman Nippon, B9.

177. James Studio China logo; used in conjunction with Crown Nippon mark.

178. JPL Hand Painted Nippon.

179. Kenilworth Studios Nippon.

180. Komaru symbol, Hand Painted Nippon.

181. Komaru symbol, Hand Painted Nippon No. 16034. Note: Japanese characters are fictitious.

182. M Nippon 10.

183. M Nippon, F24.

184. Manikin Nippon sticker; found on dolls.

185. Meiyo China Y in circle Nippon.

NIPPON
3

186. Nippon 3.

A3
NIPPON

187. Nippon A3.

188. Nippon 144.

189. Nippon with symbol.

190. Nippon with symbol.

191. Nippon with symbol.

192. Nippon with symbol.

193. Nippon with symbol.

194. Nippon with symbol.

195. Nippon with symbol.

196. Nippon with symbol.

197. Nippon with symbol.

198. Nippon with symbol, H in diamond, 14 B, P. 4.

199. Noritake M in wreath Nippon; M = Morimura Bros.; found in green, blue and magenta; Derby indicates pattern.

200. Noritake M in wreath Nippon; M = Morimura Bros.; Sahara indicates pattern.

201. Noritake M in wreath Nippon; M = Morimura Bros.; the Kiva indicates pattern.

202. Noritake M in wreath Nippon; M = Morimura Bros.; the Metz indicates pattern.

203. Noritake M in wreath Nippon; M = Morimura Bros. Registered in Japan in 1912.

204. Noritake M in wreath Hand Painted Nippon; M = Morimura Bros.; Marguerite indicates pattern.

205. Noritake M in wreath Hand Painted Nippon; M = Morimura Bros.; Sedan indicates pattern. 1st dinner set made in Noritake factory 1914.

206. Noritake M in wreath Hand Painted Nippon; M = Morimura Bros.; The Vitry indicates pattern.

NPMC
NIPPON
HAND PAINTED

207. NPMC Nippon Hand Painted.

208. RC Noritake Nippon; Waverly indicates pattern.

209. RE Nippon 1120.

210. RE Nippon 04.

211. RE Nippon B 9.

212. RE Made in Nippon A 4.

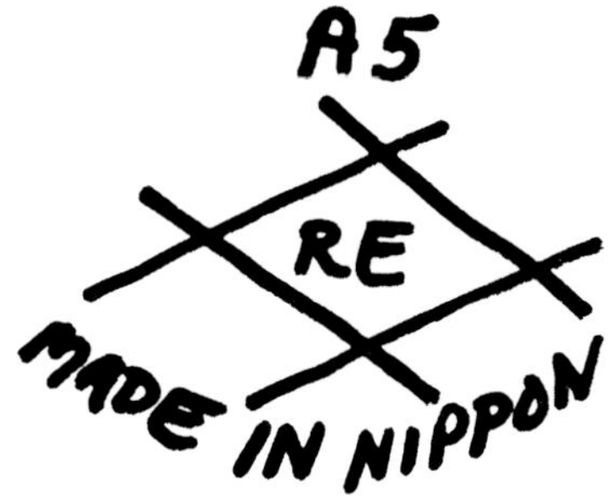


213. RE Made in Nippon A 5.

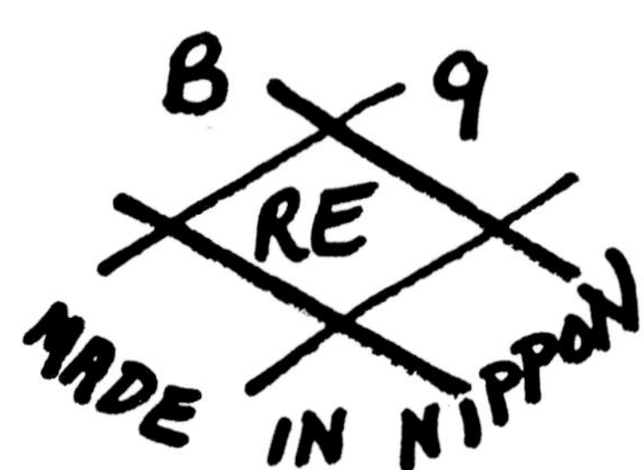


214. RE Made in Nippon B 9.

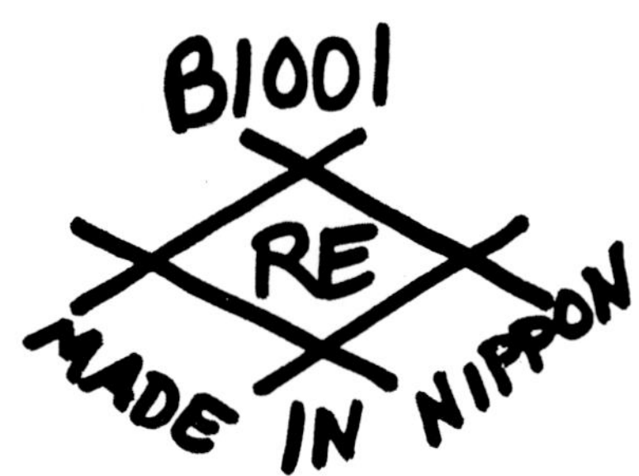

215. RE Made in Nippon B1001.

216. Royal Kuyu Nippon.

217. S in circle Nippon.

218. Sendai Hand Painted Nippon.

219. Stouffer Hand Painted Nippon.

220. Tanega Hand Painted Nippon.

221. Torii Nippon; similar to No. 113.

222. Nagoya N & Co. Nippon.

223. Old Blue Nippon.

*These marks were used during the Nippon era but may have also been used after 1921.

224* RC Noritake mark used for domestic market in Japan by Noritake Co. since 1906. The RC stands for Royal Crockery (fine china). The symbol design is called "Yajirobe" (toy of balance). It symbolizes the balance in management.

228* Noritaké, made in Japan registered in London in 1908 by Noritake Co.

225* RC Noritake mark used for domestic market in Japan by Noritake Co. since 1906. The RC stands for Royal Crockery (fine china). The symbol design is called Yajirobe (toy of balance). It symbolizes the balance in management.

229* Noritaké, registered in London in 1908 by Noritake Co.

226* RC Nippontoki-Nagoya mark used for domestic market in Japan by Noritake Co. since 1906. The RC stands for Royal Crockery (fine china).

230* Noritake, made in Japan mark registered in Japan in 1911.

227* Made in Japan mark used by Noritake Co. for export to U.S. since 1906.

231* RC Japan; Noritake Co. started using the mark in 1914. It was used on items sent to India & Southeast Asia. RC stands for Royal Crockery (fine china).

232 Coalportia Nippon.

233. FY Nippon 302; found incised on dolls.

234. FY Nippon 303; found incised on dolls.

235. FY Nippon 501; found incised on dolls.

236. No. 700 Nippon; found incised on dolls.

237. RE Made in Nippon C8; found incised on dolls.

238. RE Nippon, M18; found incised on dolls.

239. SK Made in Nippon.

特許
第一七七〇五號
PATENT
NO.17705.
FEB.26.1910
ROYAL.KINJO
JAPAN

240. Patent No. 17705 Royal Kinjo.

241. RS Japan; found on coralene pieces.

U.S.PATENT
NBR.912171.
FEB.9.1909
特許
第一六一三七號
JAPAN

242. U.S. Patent 912171; found on coralene pieces.

243. U.S. Patent 912171; found on coralene pieces.

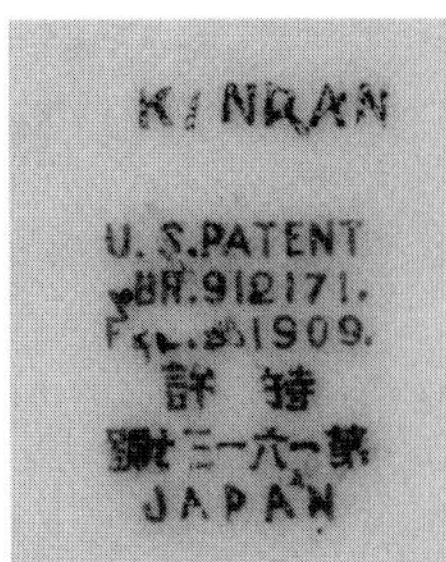


244. Kinran U.S. Patent 912171; found on coralene pieces.

245. Patent applied for No. 38257; found on coralene pieces.

246. Kinran Patent No. 16137; found on coralene pieces.

247. FY Nippon 204; found on dolls.

248. FY Nippon 409; found on dolls.

249. FY Nippon 15/4; found on dolls.

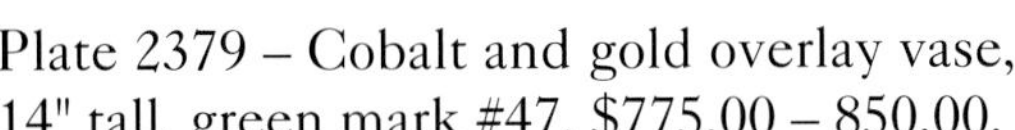

Plate 2379 – Cobalt and gold overlay vase, 14" tall, green mark #47, $775.00 – 850.00.

Plate 2380 – Cobalt and gold overlay bolted urn, 28" tall, green mark #47, $8,000.00 – 9,500.00.

Plate 2381 – Cobalt and gold overlay vase, 12½" tall, blue mark #52, $675.00 – 750.00.

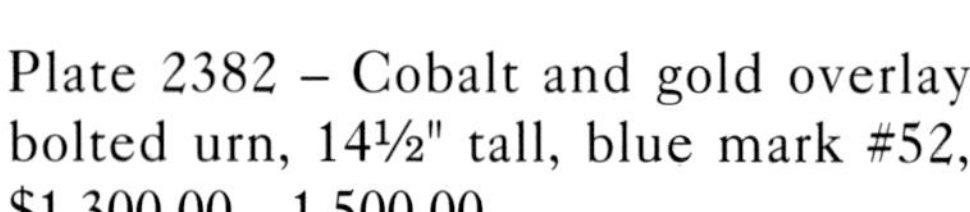

Plate 2382 – Cobalt and gold overlay bolted urn, 14½" tall, blue mark #52, $1,300.00 – 1,500.00.

Plate 2383 – Cobalt, floral and gold overlay vase, 9" tall, blue mark #52, $475.00 – 575.00.

Plate 2384 – Cobalt, floral and gold overlay vase, 9" tall, blue mark #52, $500.00 – 600.00.

Plate 2385 – Cobalt, scenic and gold overlay vase, 5" tall, blue mark #52, $325.00 – 400.00.

Plate 2386 – Cobalt, floral and gold overlay vase, 18" tall, blue mark #52, $1,800.00 – 2,200.00.

Plate 2387 – Cobalt, scenic and gold overlay vase, 12¼" tall, blue mark #52, $575.00 – 650.00.

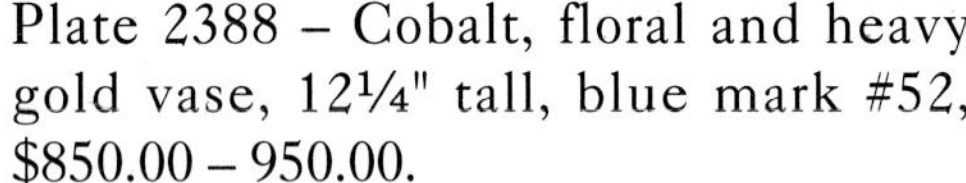

Plate 2388 – Cobalt, floral and heavy gold vase, 12¼" tall, blue mark #52, $850.00 – 950.00.

Plate 2389 – Cobalt, scenic bolted urn, 21" tall, blue mark #52, $3,200.00 – 3,600.00.

Plate 2390 – Cobalt, scenic bolted urn, 24" tall, blue mark #52, $5,500.00 – 6,500.00.

Plate 2391 – Cobalt, scenic bolted urn, 14½" tall, green mark #52, $1,500.00 – 1,800.00.

Plate 2392 – Cobalt, scenic bolted urn, 15½" tall, blue mark #47, $1,000.00 – 1,200.00.

Plate 2393 – Cobalt vase, 9" tall, mark #70, $350.00 – 425.00.

Plate 2394 – Cobalt scenic compote, 8½" tall, blue mark #52, $395.00 – 450.00.

Plate 2395 – Cobalt, scenic vase, 13½" tall, blue mark #52, $2,800.00 – 3,200.00.

Plate 2396 – Cobalt scenic vase, 8" tall, blue mark #52, $650.00 – 750.00.

Plate 2397 – Cobalt and floral coffee set, comes with four cups and saucers, blue mark #52, $350.00 – 550.00.

Plate 2398 – Cobalt and scenic chocolate set, comes with four cups and saucers, blue mark #52, $1,800.00 – 2,200.00.

Plate 2399 – Pair of cobalt and scenic vases, 7¾" tall, blue mark #52, $325.00 – 375.00 each. Middle, cobalt scenic urn, 9" tall, blue mark #52, $450.00 – 525.00.

Plate 2400 – Cobalt, gold beaded tea set, comes with six cups and saucers, unmarked, $900.00 – 1,000.00.

Plate 2401 – Cobalt, gold, floral portrait vase, 9½" tall, green mark #52, $1,300.00 – 1,500.00.

Plate 2402 – Cobalt, gold floral portrait vase, 7¾" tall, green mark #52, $900.00 – 1,000.00.

Plate 2403 – Cobalt, gold floral portrait vase, 8" tall, green mark #52, $900.00 – 1,000.00.

Plate 2404 – Cobalt, gold, floral portrait basket vase, 9¾" tall, green mark #52, $1,300.00 – 1,400.00.

Plate 2405 – Cobalt, gold, floral portrait tankard, 14½" tall, blue mark #52, $1,800.00 – 2,000.00.

Plate 2406 – Cobalt, gold, floral portrait vase, 9¾" tall, green mark #52, $1,300.00 – 1,500.00.

Plate 2407 – Cobalt, gold, floral portrait vase, 6½" tall, green mark #52, $1,000.00 – 1,100.00.

Plate 2408 – Cobalt, gold, floral portrait vase, 9½" tall, green mark #52, $1,300.00 – 1,500.00.

Plate 2409 – Portrait covered urn featuring Queen Louise, 14½" tall, blue mark #52, $2,300.00 – 2,500.00.

Plate 2410 – Portrait vase featuring Queen Louise, 12" tall, blue mark #52, $1,600.00 – 1,800.00.

Plate 2411 – Portrait vase featuring Queen Louise, 14" tall, blue mark #52, $1,700.00 – 1,900.00.

Plate 2412 – Portrait vase featuring Queen Louise, 9¼" tall, blue mark #52, $1,400.00 – 1,600.00.

Plate 2413 – Portrait bolted urn featuring Lebrun, 15¼" tall, blue mark #52, $1,500.00 – 1,700.00.

Plate 2414 – Portrait urn, 14" tall, blue mark #52, $1,200.00 – 1,350.00.

Plate 2415 – Portrait ewer featuring Lebrun, 12" tall, green mark #52, $1,250.00 – 1,400.00.

Plate 2416 – Portrait ewer featuring Madame Recamier, 12" tall, blue mark #52, $1,250.00 – 1,400.00.

Plate 2417 – Portrait vase, 8½" tall, green mark #52, $850.00 – 950.00.

Plate 2418 – Portrait vase, 8" tall, blue mark #52, $850.00 – 950.00.

Plate 2419 – Portrait vase, 11" tall, blue mark #52, $850.00 – 1,000.00.

Plate 2420 – Portrait vase, 8½" tall, unmarked, $950.00 – 1,050.00.

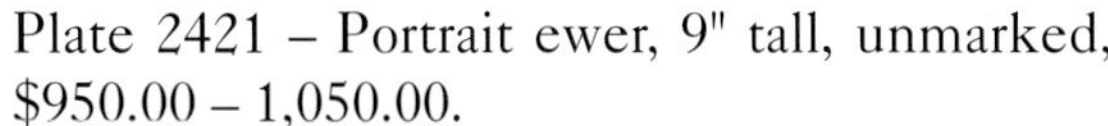

Plate 2421 – Portrait ewer, 9" tall, unmarked, $950.00 – 1,050.00.

Plate 2422 – Portrait plate, 10" wide, unmarked, $675.00 – 750.00.

Plate 2423 – Portrait plate, 10" wide, green mark #52, $675.00 – 750.00.

Plate 2424 – Portrait plate, 10" wide, green mark #52, $675.00 – 750.00.

Plate 2425 – Portrait plate, 10" wide, green mark #52, $675.00 – 750.00.

Plate 2426 – Portrait wine jug featuring the Cardinal, 9½" tall, blue mark #52, $1,800.00 – 2,100.00.

Plate 2427 – Portrait wine jug, 9½" tall, blue mark #52, $1,800.00 – 2,100.00.

Plate 2428 – Portrait wine jug, 9½" tall, green mark #52, $1,800.00 – 2,100.00.

Plate 2429 – Portrait wine jug, 9½" tall, green mark #47, $1,600.00 – 1,800.00.

Plate 2430 – Portrait mug, 5½" tall, green mark #52, $500.00 – 600.00. Portrait mug, 5½" tall, green mark #52, $500.00 – 600.00.

Plate 2431 – Portrait humidor, 8" tall, green mark #52, $1,600.00 – 1,800.00.

Plate 2432 – Portrait humidor, 8" tall, blue mark #52, $1,800.00 – 2,100.00.

Plate 2433 – Tapestry vase, 6" tall, blue mark #52, $650.00 – 750.00. Tapestry vase, 6" tall, blue mark #52, $650.00 – 750.00.

Plate 2434 – Tapestry vase, 6½" tall, blue mark #52, $625.00 – 725.00. Tapestry vase, 6" tall, blue mark #52, $625.00 – 725.00.

Plate 2435 – Tapestry humidor, 6½" tall, blue mark #52, $1,900.00 – 2,100.00. Tapestry vase, 6" tall, blue mark #52, $950.00 – 1,100.00.

Plate 2436 – Tapestry vase, 7¾" tall, blue mark #52, $750.00 – 850.00.

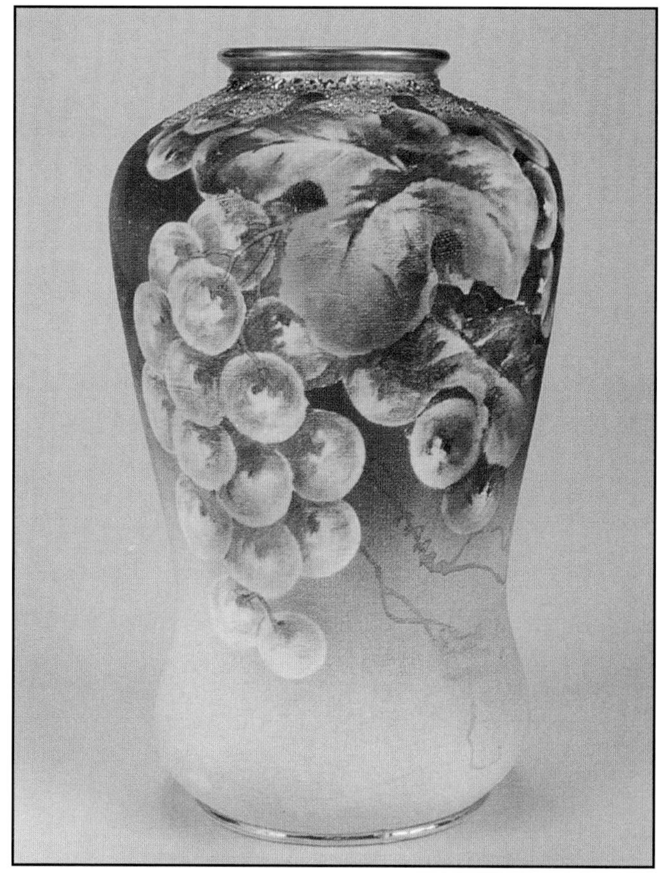

Plate 2437 – Tapestry vase, 8" tall, blue mark #52, $800.00 – 950.00.

Plate 2438 – Tapestry vase, 9½" tall, blue mark #52, $750.00 – 900.00.

Plate 2439 – Tapestry vase, 5½" tall, blue mark #52, $675.00 – 775.00.

Plate 2440 – Tapestry vase, 6¼" tall, blue mark #52, $675.00 – 775.00.

Plate 2441 – Tapestry vase, 10" tall, blue mark #52, $750.00 – 900.00.

Plate 2442 – Wedgwood-style vase, 7¾" tall, green mark #47, $550.00 – 650.00.

Plate 2443 – Wedgwood-style scenic vase, 7" tall, green mark #47, $500.00 – 600.00.

Plate 2444 – Wedgwood-style scenic loving cup, 7¾" tall, green mark #47, $500.00 – 600.00.

Plate 2445 – Wedgwood-style compote, 6¼" tall, green mark #47, $500.00 – 600.00.

Plate 2446 – Moriage vase, white woodland pattern, 8¼" tall, blue mark #47, $450.00 – 550.00. Moriage vase, white woodland pattern, 5½" tall, blue mark #47, $400.00 – 475.00.

Plate 2447 – Moriage vase, white woodland pattern, 8½" tall, green mark #47, $450.00 – 550.00.

Plate 2448 – Moriage vase, white woodland pattern, 9" tall, green mark #47, $450.00 – 550.00.

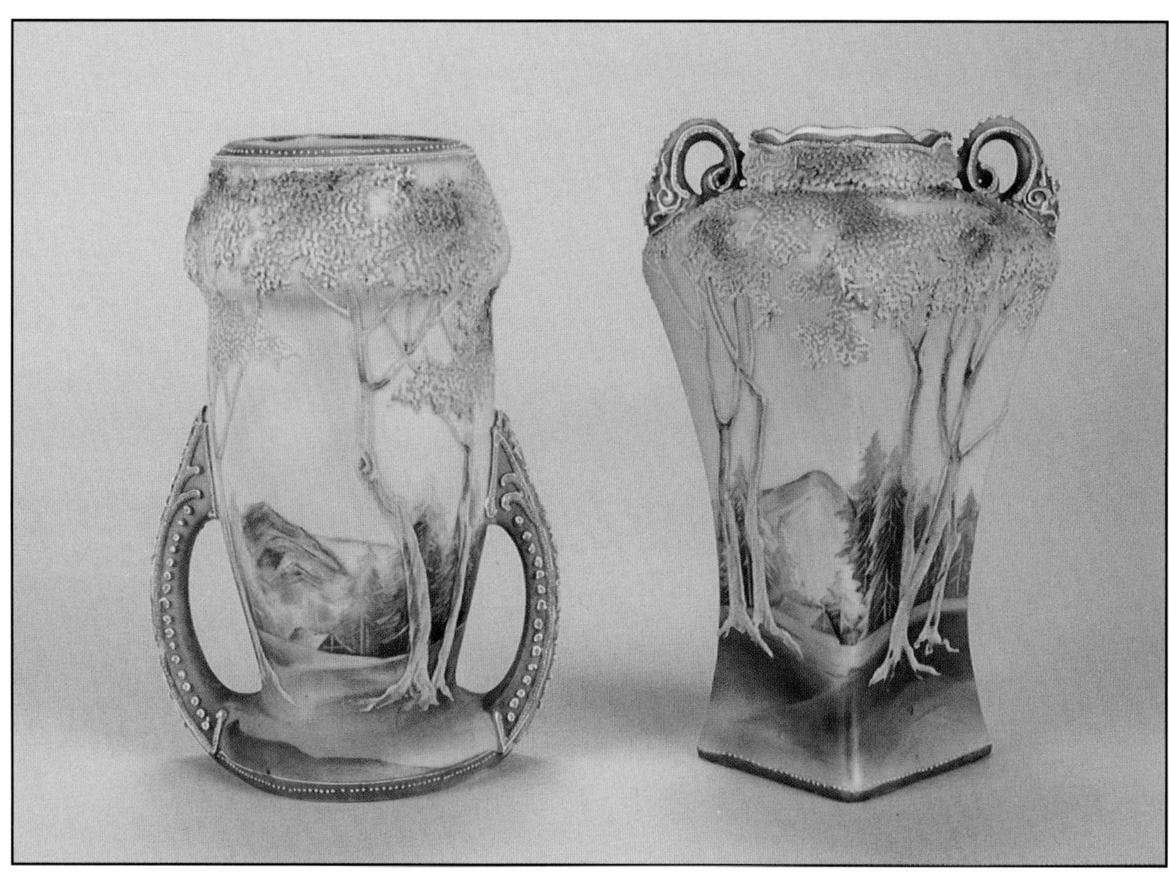

Plate 2449 – Moriage vase, white woodland pattern, 6¾" tall, blue mark #47, $400.00 – 475.00. Moriage vase, white woodland pattern, 7" tall, blue mark #47, $400.00 – 475.00.

Plate 2450 – Moriage whiskey jug, white woodland pattern, 7½" tall, blue mark #47, $750.00 – 950.00.

Plate 2451 – Moriage vase, white woodland pattern, 9" tall, green mark #47, $475.00 – 575.00.

Plate 2452 – Moriage dragon dresser set, green mark #47, $750.00 – 900.00.

Plate 2453 – Moriage dragon condensed milk container, green mark #47, $400.00 – 500.00.

Plate 2454 – Moriage dragon vase, 8" tall, blue mark #52, $325.00 – 400.00.

Plate 2455 – Moriage dragon tankard set, tankard is 14" tall, green mark #47, $2,600.00 – 2,800.00.

Plate 2456 – Moriage dragon chocolate set, green mark #47, $650.00 – 725.00. Moriage dragon cake set, green mark #47, $350.00 – 425.00.

Plate 2457 – Moriage dragon vase, 9½" tall, blue mark #52, $675.00 – 775.00.

Plate 2458 – Moriage dragon bolted urn, 11" unmarked, $375.00 – 450.00.

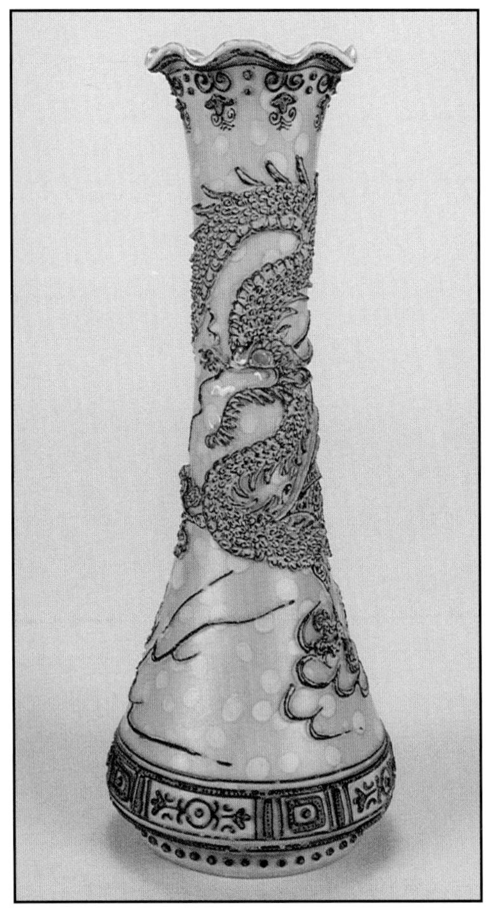

Plate 2459 – Moriage dragon vase, 15" tall, unmarked, $475.00 – 600.00.

Plate 2460 – Moriage dragon humidor, 5½" tall, blue mark #52, $425.00 – 525.00.

Plate 2461 – Moriage flying geese vase, 6½" tall, blue mark #52, $550.00 – 625.00.

Plate 2462 – Moriage flying geese tankard, 10" tall, blue mark #52, $750.00 – 850.00.

Plate 2463 – Moriage flying geese plate, 11" diameter, green mark #52, $600.00 – 700.00.

Plate 2464 – Moriage flying geese vase, 11¾" tall, blue mark #52, $825.00 – 900.00.

Plate 2465 – Moriage flying geese vase (geese flying backwards), 9" tall, blue mark #52, $650.00 – 750.00.

Plate 2466 – Moriage flying geese vase, 6½" tall, blue mark #70, $425.00 – 500.00.

Plate 2467 – Moriage flying geese basket vase, 8½" tall, unmarked, $650.00 – 725.00.

Plate 2468 – Moriage flying geese vase (geese flying backwards), 8¾" tall, green mark #90, $650.00 – 725.00.

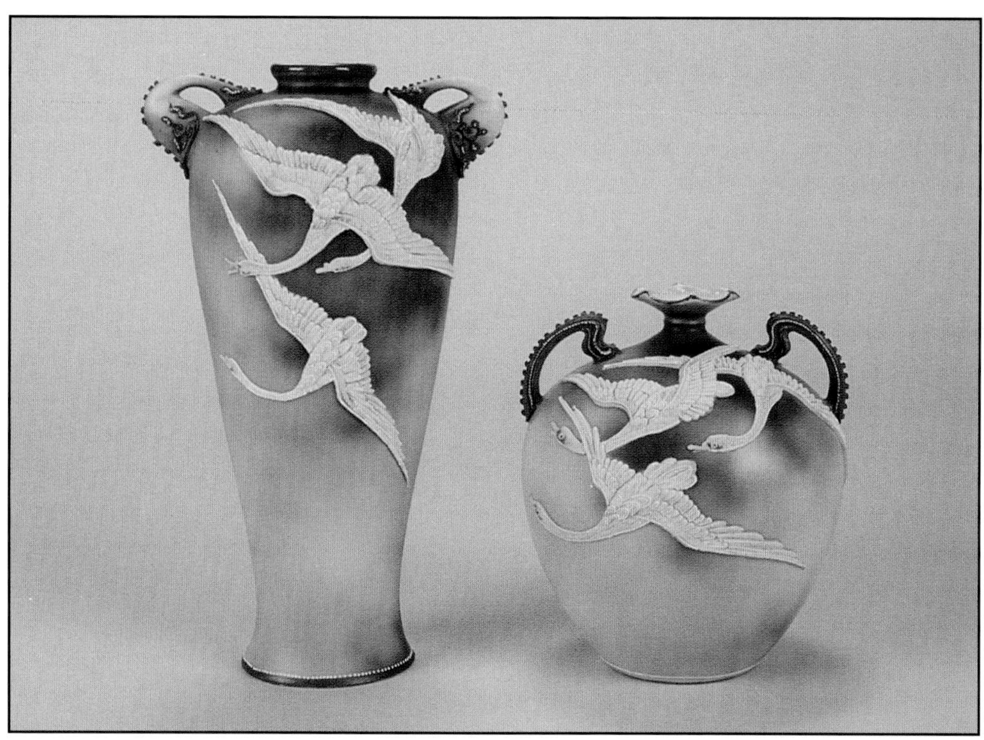

Plate 2469 – Moriage flying geese vase, 9" tall, blue mark #52, $650.00 – 750.00.
Moriage flying geese vase, 5½" tall, blue mark #52, $400.00 – 475.00.

Plate 2470 – Moriage flying geese vase, 10½" tall, blue mark #52, $650.00 – 750.00.

Plate 2471 – Moriage flying geese vase, 14" tall, blue mark #52, $800.00 – 1,000.00.

Plate 2472 – Moriage vase, 8¾" tall, green mark #52, $400.00 – 450.00.

Plate 2473 – Moriage vase, 8" tall, green mark #52, $500.00 – 550.00.

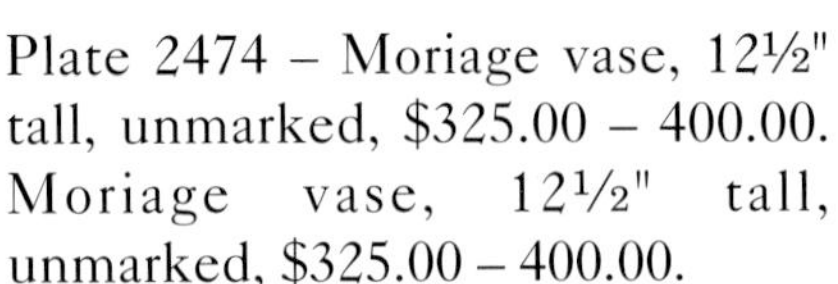

Plate 2474 – Moriage vase, 12½" tall, unmarked, $325.00 – 400.00. Moriage vase, 12½" tall, unmarked, $325.00 – 400.00.

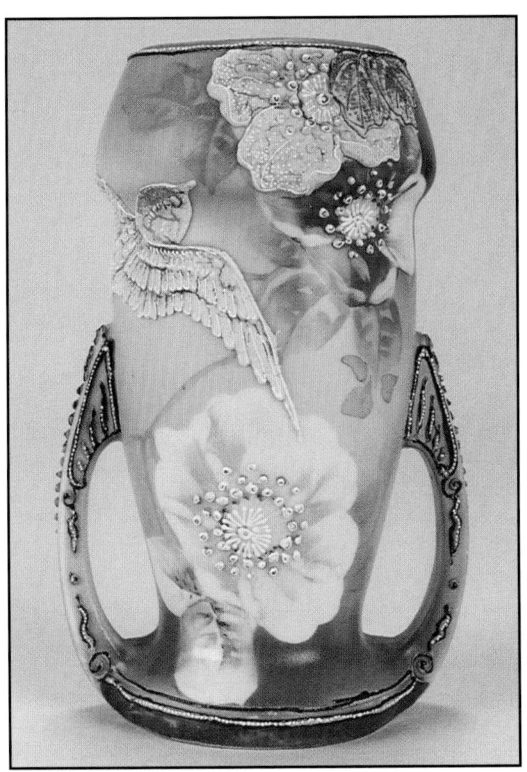

Plate 2475 – Moriage vase, 6¾" tall, blue mark #52, $350.00 – 425.00.

Plate 2476 – Moriage footed bowl, 4¾" tall, blue mark #52, $375.00 – 425.00.

Plate 2477 – Moriage vase, 8½" tall, blue mark #52, $575.00 – 625.00.

Plate 2478 – Moriage covered jar, 7" tall, blue mark #52, $600.00 – 650.00.

Plate 2479 – Moriage vase, 10½" tall, blue mark #52, $750.00 – 800.00.

Plate 2480 – Moriage vase, 10¼" tall, blue mark #52, $625.00 – 750.00.

Plate 2481 – Moriage vase, 8½" tall, blue mark #52, $1,500.00 – 1,700.00.

Plate 2482 – Moriage vase, 8½" tall, blue mark #52, $625.00 – 725.00.

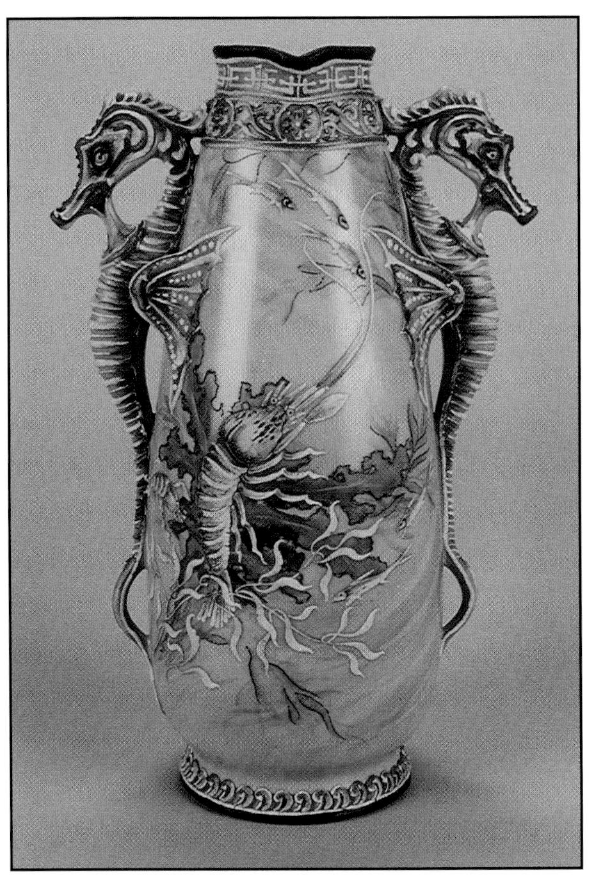

Plate 2483 – Moriage vase, seahorse handles, 11" tall, blue mark #52, $1,600.00 – 1,800.00.

Plate 2484 – Moriage vase, 6½" tall, unmarked, $300.00 – 350.00.

Plate 2486 – Moriage covered urn, 7½" tall, unmarked, $450.00 – 525.00.

Plate 2485 – Moriage bolted urn, 11¼" tall, unmarked, $600.00 – 700.00.

Plate 2487 – Moriage bolted urn, 11¼" tall, unmarked, \$475.00 – 550.00.

Plate 2488 – Moriage vase, 11¼" tall, unmarked, \$450.00 – 525.00.

Plate 2489 – Moriage basket vase, 9½" tall, unmarked, \$275.00 – 350.00.

Plate 2490 – Moriage bolted covered urn, 14" tall, unmarked, $750.00 – 850.00. Moriage bolted ewer, 12" tall, unmarked, $500.00 – 600.00.

Plate 2491 – Moriage vase, 7½" tall, unmarked, $275.00 – 350.00.

Plate 2492 – Moriage vase, 7¾" tall, unmarked, $275.00 – 325.00.

Plate 2493 – Moriage vase, 10" tall, unmarked, $325.00 – 400.00.

Plate 2494 – Moriage vase, 6¾" tall, blue mark #52, $375.00 – 425.00. Moriage vase, 8" tall, blue mark #52, $425.00 – 475.00.

Plate 2495 – Moriage vase, 8" tall, blue mark #52, $275.00 – 350.00.

Plate 2496 – Moriage vase, 10½" tall, unmarked, $375.00 – 450.00.

Plate 2497 – Moriage chocolate set, pot is 9½" tall, unmarked, $675.00 – 775.00.

Plate 2498 – Moriage humidor with squirrel finial, 7½" tall, unmarked, $700.00 – 800.00.

Plate 2499 – Moriage wine jug, 8" tall, blue mark #52, $650.00 – 750.00.

Plate 2500 – Coralene portrait plaque featuring Lebrun, 8¾" wide, mark #244, $1,500.00 – 1,700.00. Coralene portrait plaque, 8¾" wide, mark #244, $1,500.00 – 1,700.00.

Plate 2501 – Coralene portrait plaque, 7½" wide, mark #244, $1,100.00 – 1,300.00.

Plate 2502 – Coralene portrait vase featuring lady with peacock, 5¾" tall, mark #244, $1,100.00 – 1,300.00.

Plate 2503 – Coralene covered urn, 14½" tall, mark #242, $1,400.00 – 1,600.00.

Plate 2504 – Coralene covered urn, 15" tall, mark #242, $1,400.00 – 1,600.00.

Plate 2505 – Coralene vase, 5" tall, mark #245, $475.00 – 550.00. Coralene vase, 6" tall, mark #242, $475.00 – 550.00.

Plate 2506 – Coralene vase, 8¼" tall, mark #245, $675.00 – 750.00. Coralene vase, 8¼" tall, mark #242, $675.00 – 750.00.

Plate 2507 – Coralene vase, 10" tall, mark #242, $1,200.00 – 1,400.00.

Plate 2508 – Coralene compote, 9¼" tall, mark #242, $900.00 – 1,100.00.

Plate 2509 – Coralene vase, 12¼" tall, mark #242, $700.00 – 800.00.

Plate 2510 – Coralene vase, 7½" tall, mark #242, $425.00 – 500.00. Coralene vase, 9" tall, mark #245, $575.00 – 650.00. Coralene vase, 7½" tall, mark #242, $425.00 – 500.00.

Plate 2511 – Coralene vase, 7¼" tall, mark #242, $700.00 – 800.00.

Plate 2512 – Coralene vase, 11" tall, mark #244, $750.00 – 900.00.

Plate 2513 – Coralene vase, 6¾" tall, mark #242, $375.00 – 450.00. Coralene vase, 9" tall, mark #244, $650.00 – 750.00. Coralene vase, 5¾" tall mark #242, $325.00 – 375.00.

Plate 2514 – Coralene vase, 10½" tall, mark #242, $550.00 – 650.00.

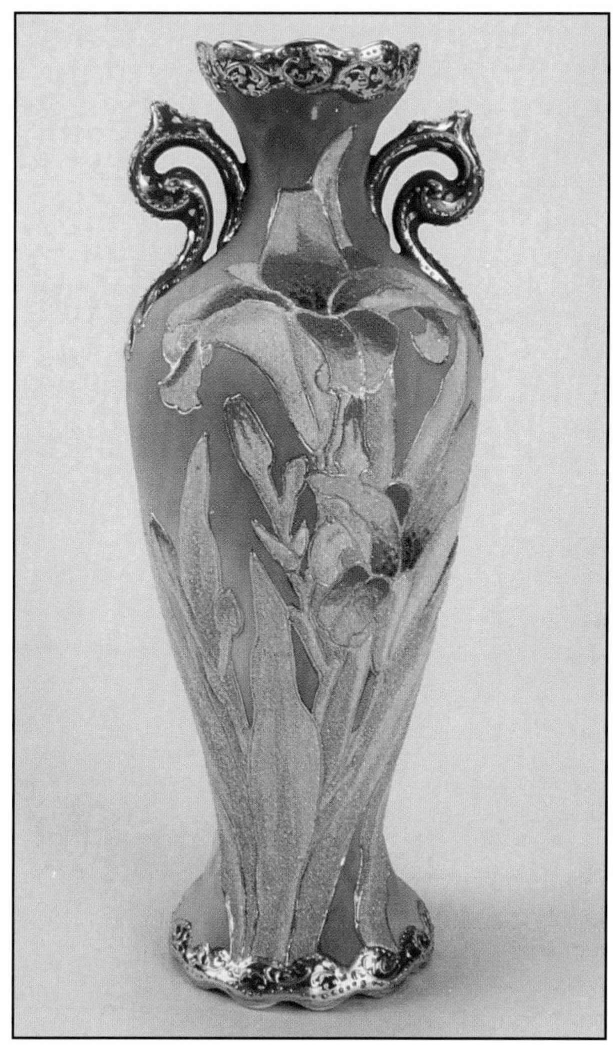

Plate 2515 – Coralene vase, 10¾" tall, mark #242, $900.00 – 1,000.00.

Plate 2516 – Coralene vase, 6½" tall, mark #245, $375.00 – 450.00. Coralene vase, 6½" tall, mark #243, $375.00 – 450.00. Coralene vase, 9½" tall, mark #244, $425.00 – 475.00.

Plate 2517 – Coralene vase, 4½" tall, mark #242, $325.00 – 375.00. Coralene vase, 10" tall, mark #243, $575.00 – 650.00. Coralene vase, 6½" tall, mark #242, $375.00 – 425.00.

Plate 2518 – Coralene vase, 10" tall, mark #244, $850.00 – 950.00.

Plate 2519 – Coralene vase, 6" tall, mark #245, $375.00 – 425.00.

Plate 2520 – Coralene vase, 8¾" tall, mark #242, $700.00 – 800.00.

Plate 2521 – Coralene vase, 10¾" tall, mark #245, $750.00 – 850.00.

Plate 2522 – Coralene vase, 8" tall, mark #242, $450.00 – 550.00. Coralene vase, 7" tall, mark #242, $450.00 – 550.00. Coralene vase, 8¼" tall, mark #242, $450.00 – 550.00.

Plate 2523 – Coralene vase, 8" tall, mark #244, $450.00 – 550.00.

Plate 2524 – Coralene vase, 6" tall, mark #242, $400.00 – 500.00.

Plate 2525 – Coralene vase, 13½" tall, mark #242, $950.00 – 1,100.00.

Plate 2526 – Coralene vase, 7" tall, mark #245, $575.00 – 650.00. Coralene vase, 7¾" tall, mark #242, $575.00 – 650.00.

Plate 2527 – Coralene vase, 5" tall, mark #245, $375.00 – 450.00. Coralene vase, 5½" tall, mark #242, $400.00 – 475.00. Coralene vase, 4¾" tall, mark #242, $325.00 – 400.00.

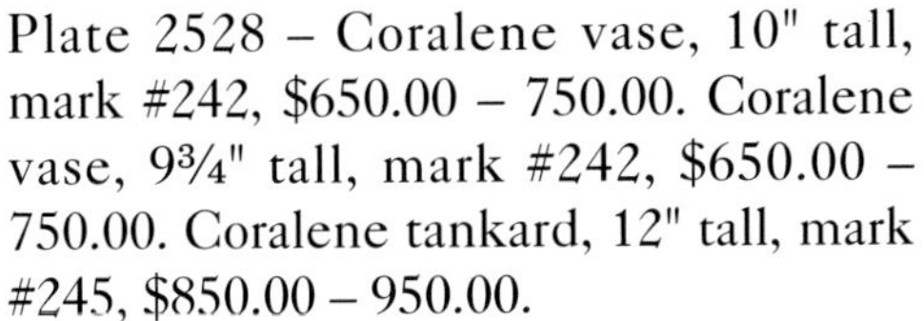

Plate 2528 – Coralene vase, 10" tall, mark #242, $650.00 – 750.00. Coralene vase, 9¾" tall, mark #242, $650.00 – 750.00. Coralene tankard, 12" tall, mark #245, $850.00 – 950.00.

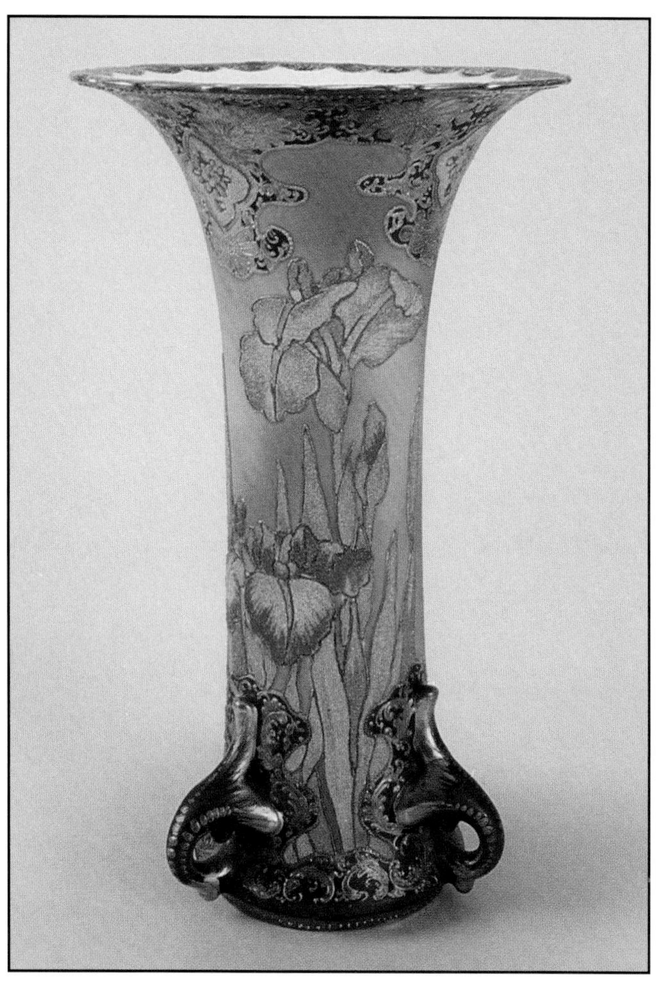

Plate 2529 – Coralene vase, 14" tall, mark #242, \$1,500.00 – 1,700.00.

Plate 2530 – Coralene vase, 10" tall, mark #245, \$750.00 – 850.00.

Plate 2531 – Coralene vase, 9" tall, mark #244, \$425.00 – 500.00. Coralene ewer, 9½" tall, mark #242, \$425.00 – 500.00.

Plate 2532 – Coralene vase, 5" tall, mark #242, $400.00 – 450.00. Coralene vase, 4" tall, mark #243, $350.00 – 400.00. Coralene vase, 3" tall, mark #243, $350.00 – 400.00.

Plate 2533 – Coralene vase, 10" tall, mark #242, $1,000.00 – 1,200.00.

Plate 2534 – Coralene vase, 9¾" tall, mark #244, $850.00 – 1,100.00.

Plate 2535 – Coralene vase, 8¼" tall, mark #242, $550.00 – 625.00. Coralene vase, 8½" tall, mark #242, $550.00 – 625.00.

Plate 2536 – Coralene vase, 6¾" tall, mark #246, $425.00 – 475.00.

Plate 2537 – Coralene ewer, 10¼" tall, mark #242, $750.00 – 850.00. Coralene vase, 10½" tall, mark #242, $700.00 – 800.00.

Plate 2538 – Coralene vase, 9¼" tall, mark #242, $450.00 – 550.00. Coralene vase, 9¼" tall, mark #242, $450.00 – 550.00.

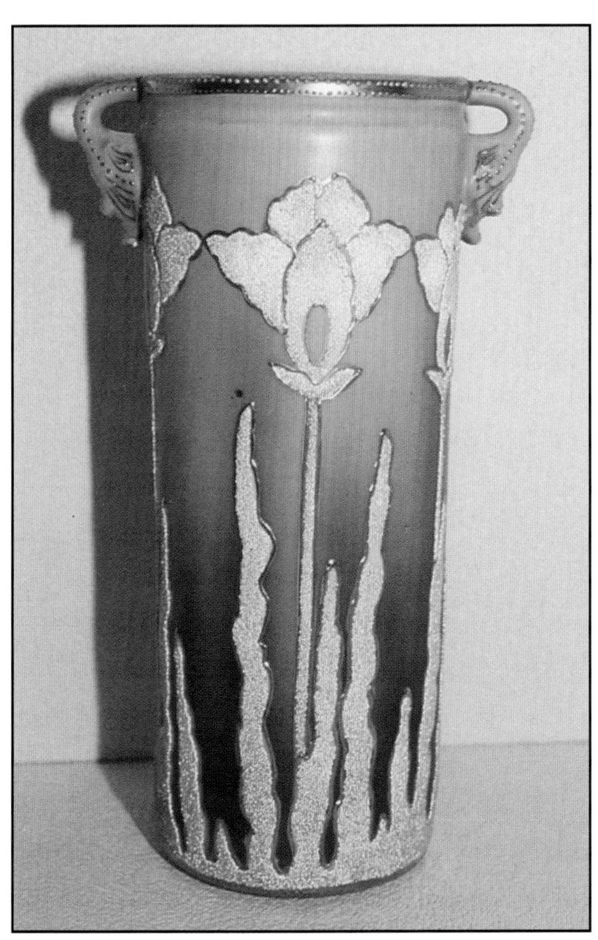

Plate 2539 – Coralene vase, 8½" tall, mark #244, $400.00 – 475.00.

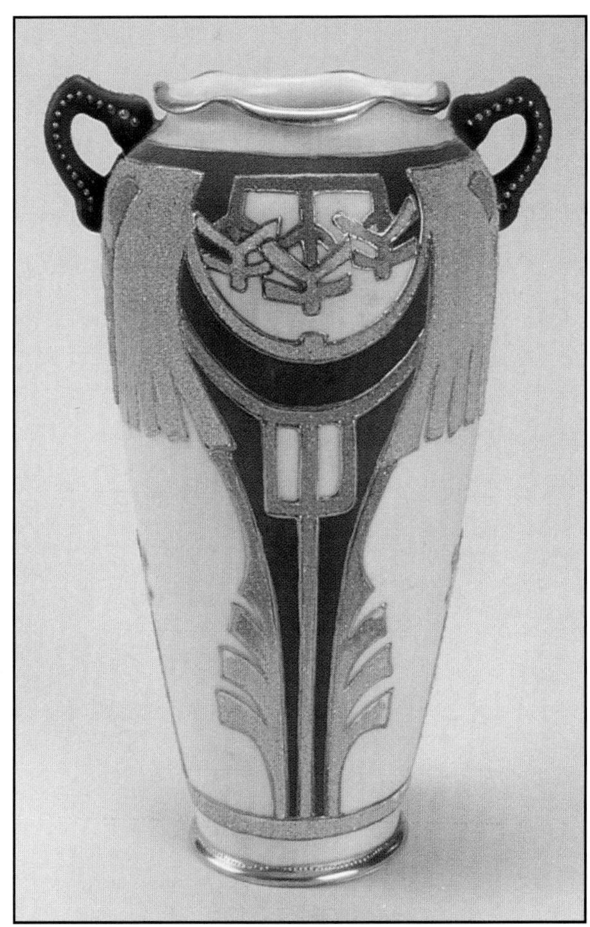

Plate 2540 – Coralene vase, 9" tall, mark #244, $750.00 – 850.00.

Plate 2541 – Coralene vase, 8¾" tall, mark #244, $450.00 – 550.00. Coralene vase, 12½" tall, mark #242, $750.00 – 850.00.

Plate 2542 – Coralene urn, 16¾" tall, mark #242, $1,200.00 – 1,400.00.

Plate 2543 – Coralene vase, 9¼" tall, mark #242, $750.00 – 825.00.

Plate 2544 – Coralene vase, 11" tall, mark #242, $1,100.00 – 1,300.00.

Plate 2545 – Coralene vase, 7" tall, mark #242, $675.00 – 750.00.

Plate 2546 – Coralene vase, 8¾" tall, mark #242, $750.00 – 850.00.

Plate 2547 – Coralene vase, 6¼" tall, mark #242, $675.00 – 750.00.

Plate 2548 – Coralene vase, 10" tall, mark #244, $750.00 – 850.00.

Plate 2549 – Coralene vase, 9" tall, mark #242, $650.00 – 750.00.

Plate 2550 – Coralene vase, 12½" tall, mark #242, $750.00 – 850.00.

Plate 2551 – Coralene vase, 9" tall, mark #242, $750.00 – 850.00.

Plate 2552 – Coralene vase, 5" tall, mark #242, $400.00 – 450.00. Coralene vase, 8¼" tall, mark #242, $600.00 – 700.00.

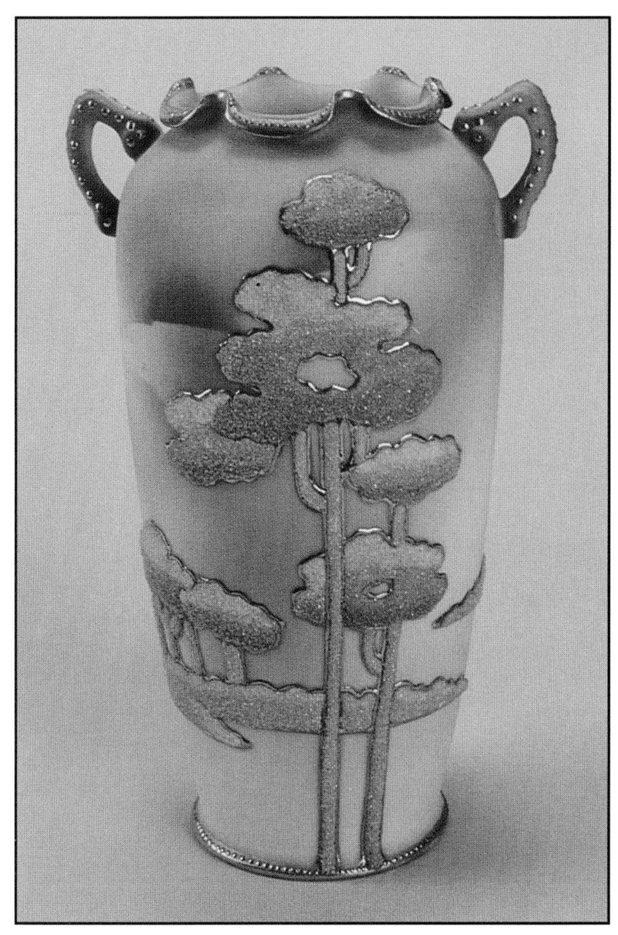

Plate 2553 – Coralene vase, 7½" tall, mark #242, $575.00 – 650.00.

Plate 2554 – Coralene vase, 8½" tall, mark #244, $1,000.00 – 1,200.00.

Plate 2555 – Coralene vases, 12¼" tall, mark #242, $625.00 – 700.00 each.

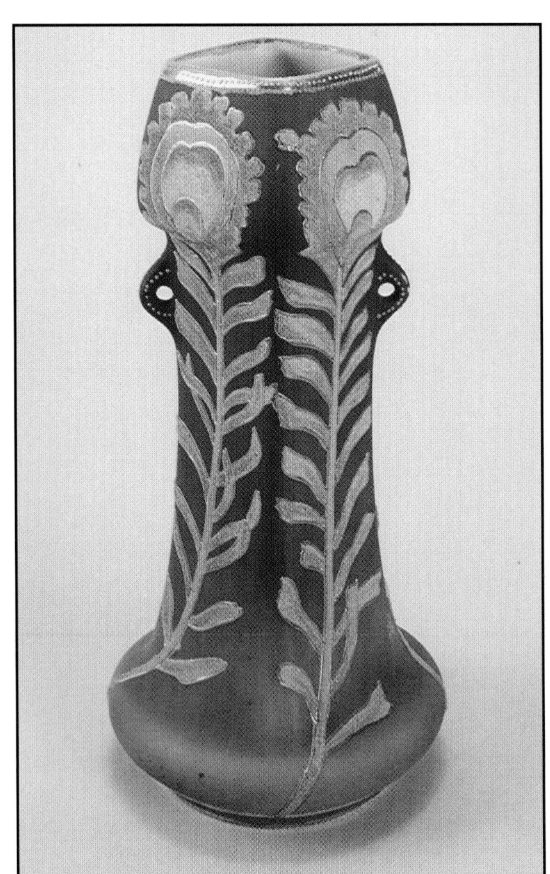

Plate 2556 – Coralene vase, 11¾" tall, mark #242, $750.00 – 850.00.

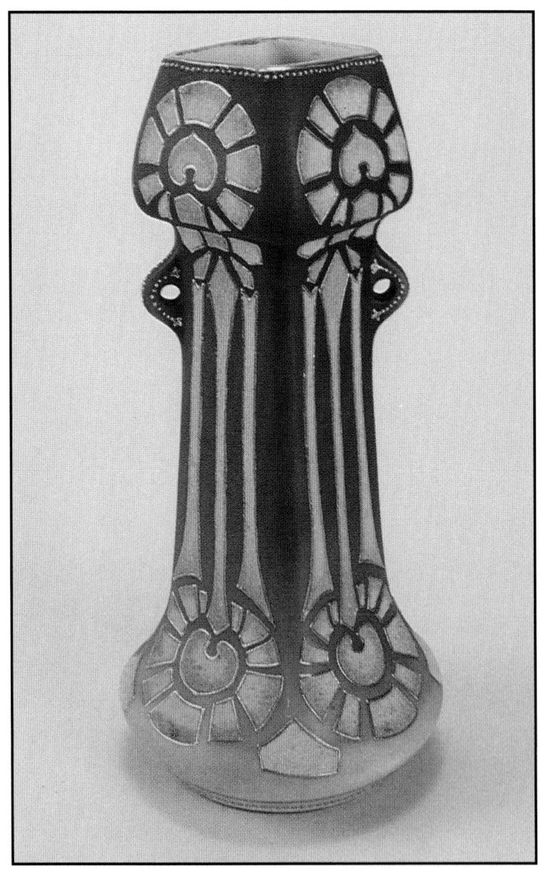

Plate 2557 – Coralene vase, 13½" tall, mark #242, $850.00 – 950.00.

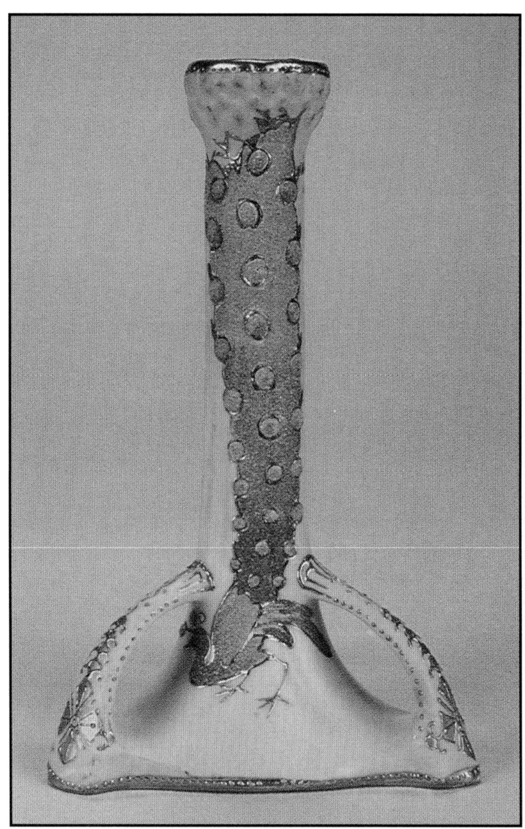

Plate 2558 – Coralene vase, 8" tall, mark #242, $750.00 – 850.00.

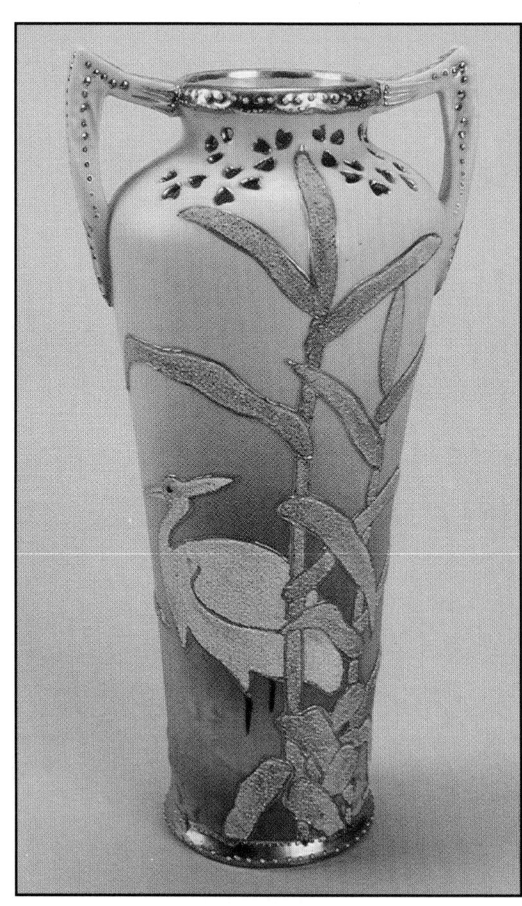

Plate 2559 – Coralene vase, 10" tall, mark #242, $750.00 – 850.00.

Plate 2560 – Coralene vase, 7" tall, mark #242, $400.00 – 450.00.

Plate 2561 – Coralene vase, 6½" tall, mark #242, $400.00 – 450.00.

Plate 2562 – Coralene bowl, 8½" tall, mark #242, $500.00 – 550.00.

Plate 2563 – Coralene vase, 9½" tall, mark #242, $650.00 – 750.00.

Plate 2564 – Coralene vase, 9" tall, mark #242, $650.00 – 750.00.

Plate 2565 – Coralene cracker jar, 6¾" tall, has original paper label "Nagoya Sample," mark #242, $900.00 – 1,050.00.

Plate 2566 – Coralene compote, 8¾" tall, mark #242, $750.00 – 850.00.

Plate 2567 – Coralene tankard, 13¼" tall, mark #242, $900.00 – 1,050.00.

Plate 2568 – Coralene vase, 7" tall, mark #242, $400.00 – 450.00. Coralene vase, 8" tall, mark #242, $475.00 – 550.00.

Plate 2569 – Coralene vase, 9½" tall, mark #242, $850.00 – 950.00.

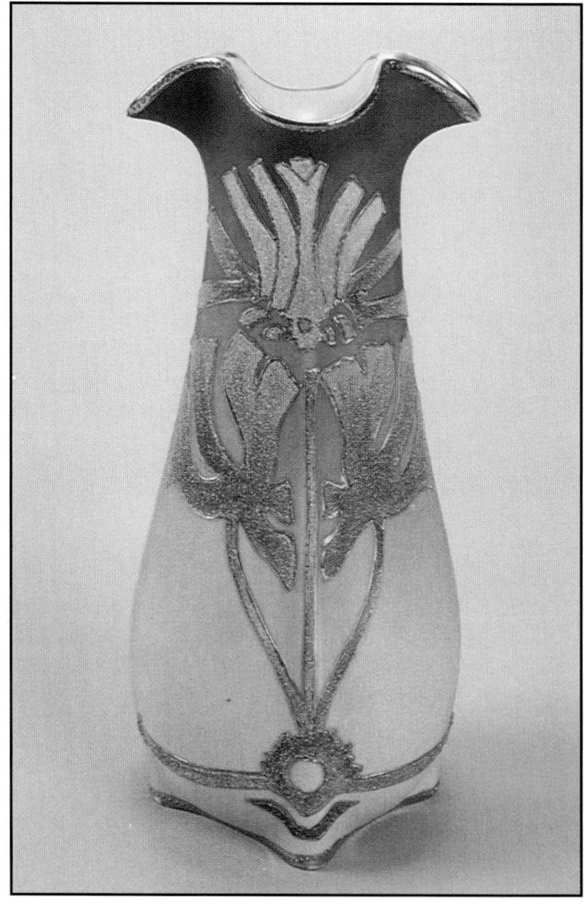

Plate 2570 – Coralene vase, 10" tall, mark #242, $700.00 – 800.00.

Plate 2571 – Coralene vase, 9¼" tall, mark #246, $650.00 – 750.00.

Plate 2572 – Coralene vase, 8½" tall, mark #242, $575.00 – 650.00.

Plate 2573 – Coralene vase, 4¼" tall, mark #243, $550.00 – 625.00.

Plate 2574 – Coralene vase, 5½" tall, mark #245, $450.00 – 550.00. Coralene vase, 9" tall, mark #245, $550.00 – 625.00.

Plate 2575 – Coralene vase, 6" tall, mark #242, $575.00 – 650.00.

Plate 2576 – Coralene vase, 7" tall, mark #242, $550.00 – 650.00.

Plate 2577 – Coralene vase, 8¾" tall, mark #242, $400.00 – 475.00. Coralene vase, 8¾" tall, mark #242, $425.00 – 500.00.

Plate 2578 – Coralene vase, 15¼" tall, mark #242, $950.00 – 1,100.00

Plate 2579 – Coralene vase, 12½" tall, mark #244, $650.00 – 750.00.

Plate 2580 – Coralene compote, 8¼" tall, mark #242, $850.00 – 1,000.00.

Plate 2581 – Coralene vase, 9¾" tall, mark #242, $700.00 – 800.00.

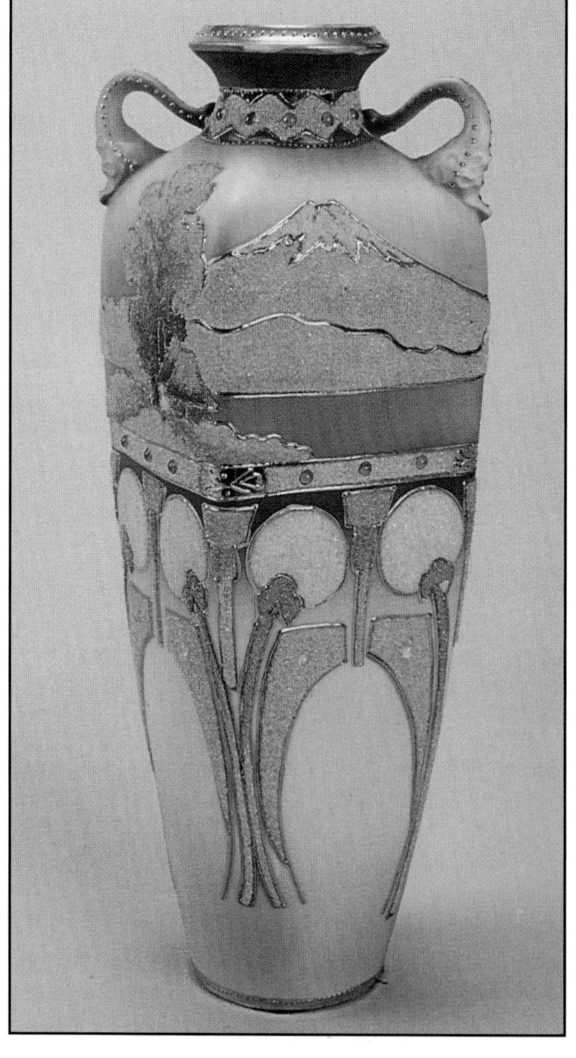

Plate 2582 – Coralene vase with jeweling, 10¾" tall, mark #244, $1,200.00 – 1,400.00.

Plate 2583 – Coralene plaque, 7½" wide, mark #242, $475.00 – 575.00. Coralene plaque, 7½" wide, mark #242, $475.00 – 575.00.

Plate 2584 – Coralene plaque, 9¾" wide, mark #242, $525.00 – 600.00.

Plate 2585 – Coralene plaque, 7½" wide, mark #242, $475.00 – 575.00.

Plate 2586 – Coralene dresser set, mark #244, $1,250.00 – 1,450.00.

Plate 2587 – Coralene tea set (creamer is missing), mark #244, $1,500.00 – 1,700.00.

Plate 2588 – Figural compote supported by three griffins, 5" tall, green mark #47, $475.00 – 575.00.

Plate 2589 – Figural compote supported by three griffins, 5" tall, green mark #47, $475.00 – 575.00.

Plate 2590 – Figural bird, 4" tall, mark #47, $250.00 – 300.00. Figural bird, 4" tall, mark #47, $250.00 – 300.00. Figural bird, 4" tall, mark #47, $250.00 – 300.00. Figural bird napkin ring, 3½" tall, mark #47, $500.00 – 600.00.

Plate 2591 – Figural dish, 2¾" wide, mark #84, $225.00 – 275.00.

Plate 2592 – Figural ashtray, 7" wide, green mark #47, $800.00 – 900.00.

Plate 2593 – Figural ashtray, 6½" wide, similar to #595 (different scene), green mark #47, $500.00 – 600.00.

Plate 2594 – Molded in relief bookends, 6" tall, green mark #47, $1,800.00 – 2,100.00 a pair.

Plate 2595 – Molded in relief humidor, 6" tall, green mark #47, similar to Plate 109, $1,000.00 – 1,200.00.

Plate 2596 – Humidor, 6" tall, green mark #47, $4,500.00 – 5,000.00.

Plate 2597 – Molded in relief humidor, 6½" tall, features the same gargoyle shown on the ashtray in Plates 2597B and 1541. It also has another gargoyle with huge teeth eating another animal, a frontal view of an elephant with tusks, a side view of an eagle eating grapes, a happy looking gargoyle holding down its prey, and another eagle, this one a front view with its wings partially outstretched, green mark #47, $3,200.00 – 3,500.00.

Plate 2597A – Different view of humidor shown in 2597.

Plate 2597B – Humidor in 2597 shown with matching ashtray (also shown in plate 1541).

Plate 2598 – Molded in relief wall plaque, 9" x 12", green mark #47, $8,500.00 – 9,500.00.

Plate 2598A – Close-up of fisherman shown in Plate 2598.

Plate 2599 – Molded in relief stein, 7" tall, green mark #47, $1,200.00 – 1,400.00.

Plate 2600 – Molded in relief vase, 10¾" tall, green mark #47, $1,800.00 – 2,200.00.

Plate 2601 – Molded in relief Egyptian style items: Letter box, 5½" long, 3" tall (same as 1504), green mark #47, $1,600.00 – 1,800.00. Letter holder, 4" tall, 5½" long, green mark #47, $1,400.00 – 1,600.00. Inkwell, 3½" tall (same as 1503), green mark #47, $1,000.00 – 1,100.00. Humidor, 6" tall, blue mark #52, $2,000.00 – 2,200.00.

Plate 2601A – Different view of humidor shown in Plate 2601. Close up view of letter holder shown in Plate 2601.

Plate 2602 – Silver overlay vase, 9½" tall, green mark #79, $750.00 – 850.00.

Plate 2603 – Silver overlay vase, 7½" tall, magenta mark #82, $900.00 – 1,000.00.

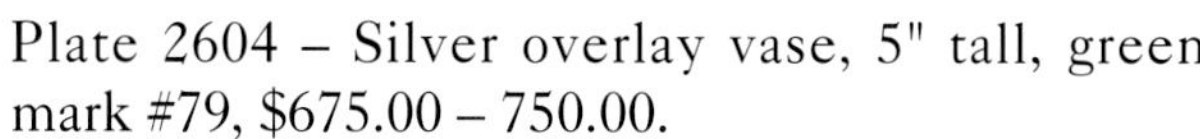

Plate 2604 – Silver overlay vase, 5" tall, green mark #79, $675.00 – 750.00.

Plate 2605 – Heavily beaded vase, 9½" tall, unmarked, $425.00 – 500.00.

Plate 2606 – Heavily beaded vase, 4½" tall, blue mark #89, $275.00 – 350.00.

Plate 2607 – Heavily beaded basket vase, 7½" tall, unmarked, $400.00 – 475.00.

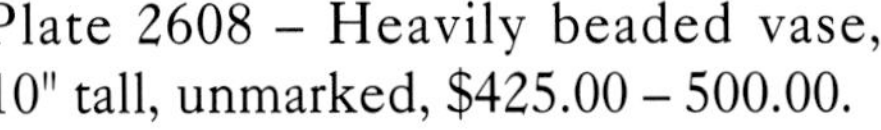

Plate 2608 – Heavily beaded vase, 10" tall, unmarked, $425.00 – 500.00.

Plate 2609 – Souvenir items of Washington, D.C.: Bowl, 7" wide, red mark #47, $75.00 – 100.00. Nappy, 5½" wide, blue mark #52, $60.00 – 85.00. Individual salt, 2¼" wide, green mark #47, $35.00 – 45.00. Pin tray, 5¼" wide, green mark #47, $60.00 – 85.00. Mustard jar, 2¾" tall, green mark #47, $60.00 – 85.00. Plate, 8¾" wide, green mark #52, $110.00 – 150.00. Nappy, 6" wide, green mark #81, $85.00 – 110.00. Bowl, 5½" wide, blue mark #38, $65.00 – 90.00. Creamer, 4½" wide, green mark #47, $35.00 – 50.00. Hatpin holder, 4¾" tall, green mark #47, $80.00 – 110.00. Sugar bowl, 3¾" tall, blue mark #38, $30.00 – 40.00.

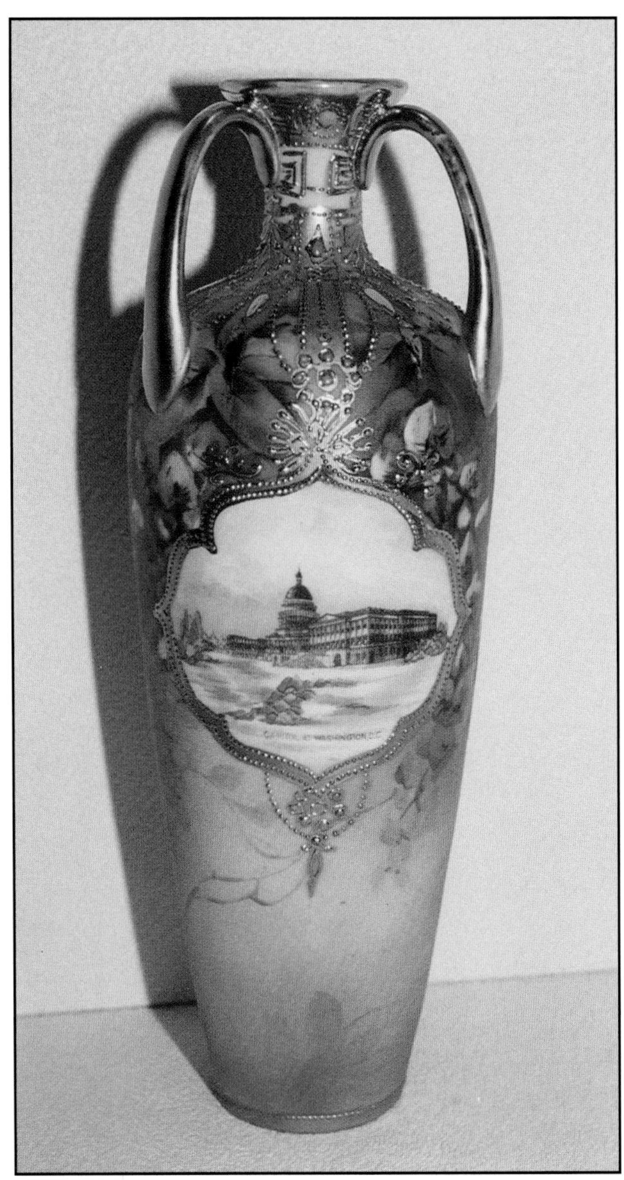

Plate 2610 – Vase, souvenir of Washington, D.C., 11½" tall, blue mark #52, $350.00 – 425.00.

Plate 2611 – Nappy, souvenir item mark #47, $100.00 – 150.00.

Plate 2612 – Ferner, hunt scene, 4" tall, blue mark #52, $400.00 – 475.00.

Plate 2613 – Stein, hunt scene, 7" tall, blue mark #52, $650.00 – 750.00.

Plate 2614 – Pitcher, hunt scene, 7" tall, blue mark #52, $425.00 – 500.00.

Plate 2615 – American Indian design bookends, molded in relief, 6" tall, green mark #47, $1,800.00 – 2,200.00 pair.

Plate 2616 – Ashtray, American Indian design featuring Sitting Bull, 5½" wide, green mark #47, $450.00 – 550.00.

Plate 2617 – Humidor, American Indian design featuring Chief Red Cloud, 4" tall, green mark #47, $550.00 – 650.00.

Plate 2618 – Humidor, American Indian design featuring Chief Red Cloud, 7½" tall, blue mark #52, $1,300.00 – 1,500.00. Humidor, American Indian design featuring Sitting Bull, 7½" wide, blue mark #52, $1,300.00 – 1,500.00.

Plate 2619 – Vase, American Indian design, 8½" tall, blue mark #38, $350.00 – 400.00.

Plate 2620 – Humidor, American Indian design adapted from Frederic Remington's *Shadows at the Waterhole*, 7" tall, green mark #47, $950.00 – 1,100.00.

Plate 2621 – Smoke set, man on camel design, green mark #47, $1,300.00 – 1,500.00.

Plate 2622 – Bolted urn, man on camel design, 18" tall, green mark #47, $1,600.00 – 1,800.00.

Plate 2623 – Humidor, man on camel design, 7" tall, green mark #47, $750.00 – 850.00.

Plate 2624 – Bolted urn, man on camel design, 28" tall, green mark #47, $7,500.00 – 8,500.00.

Plate 2625 – Bolted urn, man on camel scene, 16" tall, green mark #47, $1,600.00 – 1,800.00.

Plate 2626 – Tankard set, man on camel design, comes with six mugs, tankard is 11" tall, mugs are 4" tall, green mark #47, $1,800.00 – 2,200.00.

Plate 2627 – Vase, man on camel design, 9¼" tall, green mark #47, $500.00 – 600.00.

Plate 2628 – Wine jug, man on camel design, 9¼" tall, green mark #47, $900.00 – 1,100.00.

Plate 2629 – Vase, man on camel design, 7" tall, green mark #47, \$375.00 – 425.00. Vase, man on camel design, 6" tall, green mark #47, \$325.00 – 375.00.

Plate 2630 – Vase, man on camel design, 8" tall, green mark #47, \$425.00 – 500.00.

Plate 2631 – Vase, man on camel design, 10½" tall, green mark #47, \$475.00 – 550.00.

Plate 2632 – Dresser set, woodland scene, green mark #47, $950.00 – 1,100.00.

Plate 2633 – Vase, woodland scene, 10½" tall, blue mark #47, $575.00 – 650.00. Cracker jar, woodland scene, 8" tall, green mark #47, $575.00 – 650.00.

Plate 2634 – Chocolate set, woodland scene, comes with six cups and saucers, green mark #47, $1,100.00 – 1,300.00.

Plate 2635 – Tankard set, woodland scene, comes with six mugs, tankard is 14" tall, mugs are 4" tall, green mark #47, $3,200.00 – 3,500.00.

Plate 2636 – Cake set, woodland scene, green mark #47, $475.00 – 550.00.

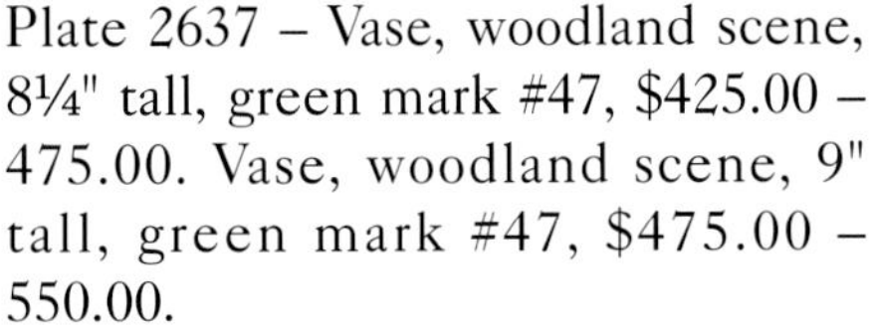

Plate 2637 – Vase, woodland scene, 8¼" tall, green mark #47, $425.00 – 475.00. Vase, woodland scene, 9" tall, green mark #47, $475.00 – 550.00.

Plate 2638 – Tea set, woodland scene, green mark #47, $650.00–750.00.

Plate 2639 – Tea set, woodland scene, blue mark #52, $900.00 – 1,100.00.

Plate 2640 – Vase, woodland scene, 8" tall, blue mark #52, $475.00 – 550.00. Vase, woodland scene, 8¼" tall, blue mark #52, $475.00 – 550.00.

Plate 2641 – Pair of candlesticks, woodland scene, 9¼" tall, green mark #47, $1,100.00 – 1,300.00.

Plate 2642 – Pitcher, woodland scene, 5¼" tall, blue mark #52, $400.00 – 450.00. Pitcher, woodland scene, 4¾" tall, blue mark #52, $400.00 – 450.00.

Plate 2643 – Vase, woodland scene, 5" tall, green mark #47, $375.00 – 450.00. Vase, woodland scene, 7½" tall, blue mark #52, $400.00 – 475.00. Vase, woodland scene, 6" tall, blue mark #52, $375.00 – 450.00.

Plate 2644 – Bolted urn, 28" tall, green mark #47, $8,000.00 – 9,500.00.

Plate 2645 – Covered urn, 10" tall, blue mark #52, $400.00 – 475.00.

Plate 2646 – Covered urn, 14½" tall, blue mark #47, $1,200.00 – 1,400.00.

Plate 2647 – Bolted urn, 16½" tall, green mark #47, $1,500.00 – 1,700.00.

Plate 2648 – Bolted urn, 14¾" tall, blue mark #52, $1,300.00 – 1,500.00.

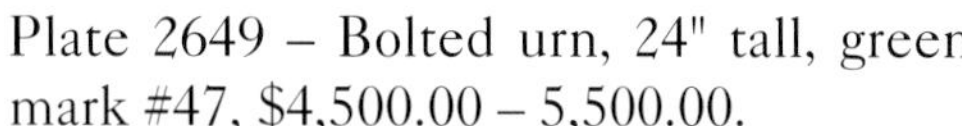

Plate 2649 – Bolted urn, 24" tall, green mark #47, $4,500.00 – 5,500.00.

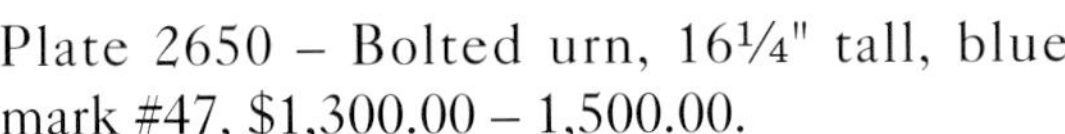

Plate 2650 – Bolted urn, 16¼" tall, blue mark #47, $1,300.00 – 1,500.00.

Plate 2651 – Covered urn, 14½" tall, blue mark #52, $1,800.00 – 2,000.00.

Plate 2652 – Pair of covered urns, 14" tall, mark #229, $1,500.00 – 1,700.00 each.

Plate 2653 – Bolted urn, 14" tall, green mark #47, $750.00 – 900.00.

Plate 2654 – Bolted urn, 15½" tall, green mark #47, $1,700.00 – 1,900.00.

Plate 2655 – Bolted urn, 14" tall, green mark #47, $900.00 – 1,100.00.

Plate 2656 – Covered urn, mark illegible, 14½" tall, $750.00 – 900.00.

Plate 2657 – Bolted urn, 15¼" tall, blue mark #52, $1,200.00 – 1,400.00.

Plate 2658 – Bolted urn, 15" tall, blue mark #52, $1,300.00 – 1,500.00.

Plate 2659 – Bolted urn, 23" tall, blue mark #47, $3,300.00 – 3,600.00.

Plate 2660 – Bolted urn, 19" tall, blue mark #52, $1,700.00 – 1,900.00.

Plate 2661 – Bolted urn, 15¼" tall, blue mark #52, $1,100.00 – 1,250.00.

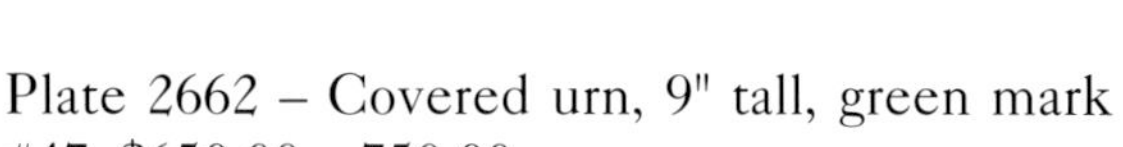

Plate 2662 – Covered urn, 9" tall, green mark #47, $650.00 – 750.00.

Plate 2663 – Covered urn, 13½" tall, unmarked, \$900.00 – 1,100.00.

Plate 2664 – Bolted urn, 16½" tall, green mark #47, \$1,400.00 – 1,600.00.

Plate 2665 – Covered urn, 24" tall, blue mark #52, $5,000.00 – 5,500.00.

Plate 2666 – Vase, 8¾" tall, green mark #52, $250.00 – 300.00. Covered urn, 10¾" tall, blue mark #52, $550.00 – 650.00. Vase, 6¼" tall, blue mark #52, $200.00 – 250.00.

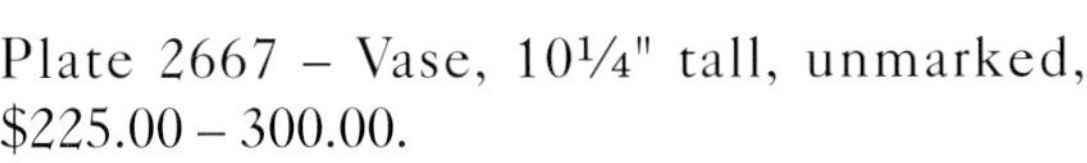

Plate 2667 – Vase, 10¼" tall, unmarked, $225.00 – 300.00.

Plate 2668 – Vase, 15¼" tall, green mark #52, $650.00 – 750.00.

Plate 2669 – Vase, 15½" tall, blue mark #52, $775.00 – 900.00.

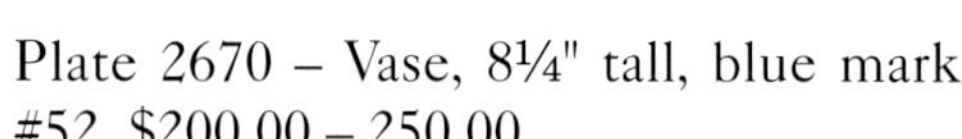

Plate 2670 – Vase, 8¼" tall, blue mark #52, $200.00 – 250.00.

Plate 2671 – Vase, 11½" tall, green mark #47, $275.00 – 325.00.

Plate 2672 – Vase, 11½" tall, blue mark #52, $425.00 – 500.00.

Plate 2673 – Vase, 15½" tall, blue mark #47, $750.00 – 825.00.

Plate 2674 – Vase, 12" tall, mark removed, $650.00 – 750.00.

Plate 2675 – Vase, 12" tall, green mark #47, $275.00 – 350.00.

Plate 2676 – Vase, 8½" tall, mark #4, $235.00 – 285.00.

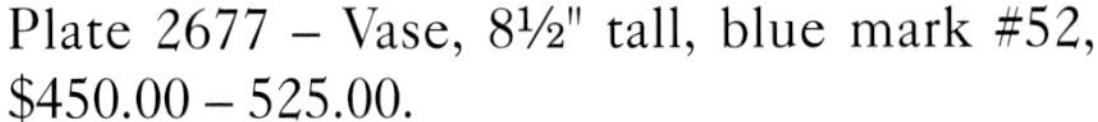

Plate 2677 – Vase, 8½" tall, blue mark #52, $450.00 – 525.00.

Plate 2678 – Vase, 10" tall, green mark #52, $300.00 – 350.00.

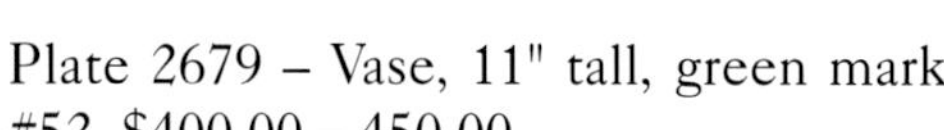

Plate 2679 – Vase, 11" tall, green mark #52, $400.00 – 450.00.

Plate 2680 – Vase, 13" tall, green mark #47, $425.00 – 500.00.

Plate 2681 – Vase, 10" tall, blue mark #47, $325.00 – 375.00.

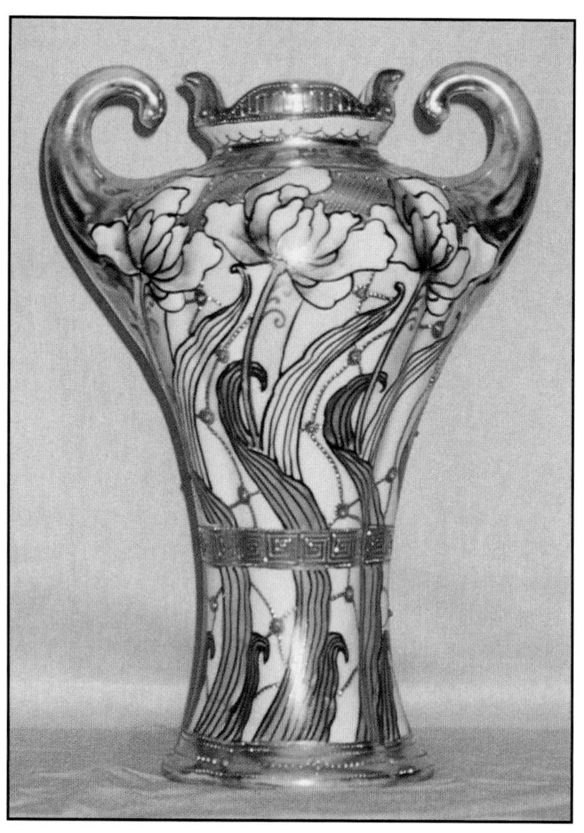

Plate 2682 – Vase, 11" tall, blue mark #52, $350.00 – 400.00.

Plate 2683 – Vase, 8" tall, green mark #47, $250.00 – 300.00.

Plate 2684 – Vase, 8½" tall, green mark #47, $400.00 – 500.00.

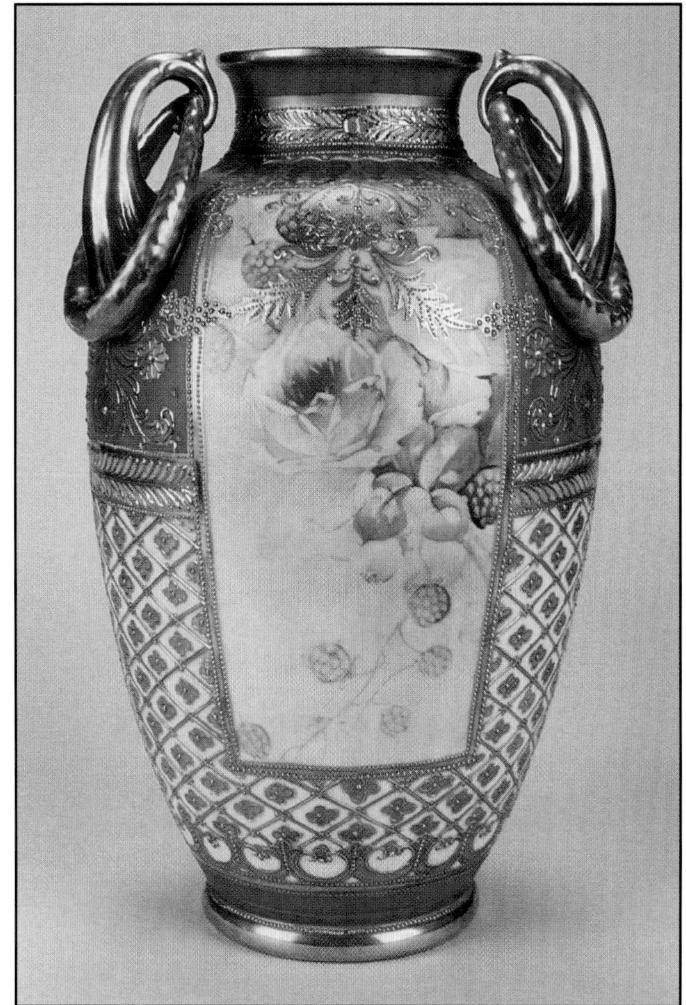

Plate 2685 – Vase, 13½" tall, blue mark #52, $1,500.00 – 1,700.00.

Plate 2686 – Vase, 14" tall, green mark #47, $1,100.00 – 1,300.00.

Plate 2687 – Vase, 12¾" tall, green mark #47, $475.00 – 550.00.

Plate 2688 – Vase, 7½" tall, green mark #47, $150.00 – 200.00.

Plate 2689 – Vase, 11¼" tall, blue mark #47, $300.00 – 375.00.

Plate 2690 – Vase, 8" tall, blue mark #47, $300.00 – 350.00.

Plate 2691 – Vase, 7" tall, green mark #47, $250.00 – 300.00.

Plate 2692 – Basket vase, 8½" tall, blue mark #52, $400.00 – 475.00.

Plate 2693 – Vase, 12" tall, blue mark #52, $600.00 – 650.00.

Plate 2694 – Vase, 12½" tall, blue mark #52, $600.00 – 650.00.

Plate 2695 – Basket vase, 10" tall, blue mark #52, $375.00 – 450.00.

Plate 2696 – Vase, 8½" tall, green mark #47, $325.00 – 375.00. Vase, 8" tall, green mark #47, $325.00 – 375.00.

Plate 2697 – Vase, 18" tall, green mark #47, $750.00 – 850.00.

Plate 2698 – Vase, 11" tall, green mark #47, $400.00 – 475.00.

Plate 2699 – Vase, 11¾" tall, green mark #47, $325.00 – 400.00.

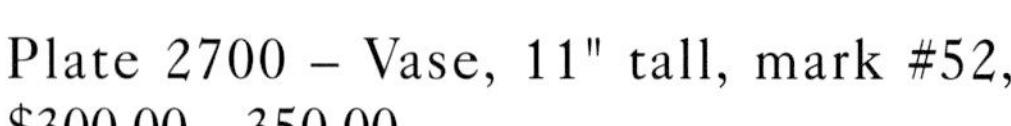

Plate 2700 – Vase, 11" tall, mark #52, $300.00 – 350.00.

Plate 2701 – Vase, 12" tall, blue mark #38, $250.00 – 325.00.

Plate 2702 – Vase, 15" tall, blue mark #47, $1,100.00 – 1,300.00.

Plate 2703 – Vase, 9" tall, mark #89, \$375.00 – 450.00. Vase, 7½" tall, mark #89, \$375.00 – 450.00.

Plate 2704 – Vase, 9" tall, blue mark #52, \$375.00 – 450.00. Vase, 8" tall, blue mark #52, \$375.00 – 450.00. Vase, 11¼" tall, blue mark #52, \$475.00 – 575.00.

Plate 2705 – Vase, 8¼" tall, blue mark #52, $200.00 – 250.00.

Plate 2706 – Vase, 11¾" tall, green mark #52, $450.00 – 550.00.

Plate 2707 – Vase, 10½" tall, blue mark #52, $350.00 – 425.00.

Plate 2708 – Vase, 14" tall, green mark #47, $650.00 – 700.00.

Plate 2709 – Vase, 9¾" tall, green mark #47, $275.00 – 325.00.

Plate 2710 – Vase, 11½" tall, green mark #47, $250.00 – 300.00.

Plate 2711 – Vase, 11½" tall, green mark #47, $350.00 – 400.00.

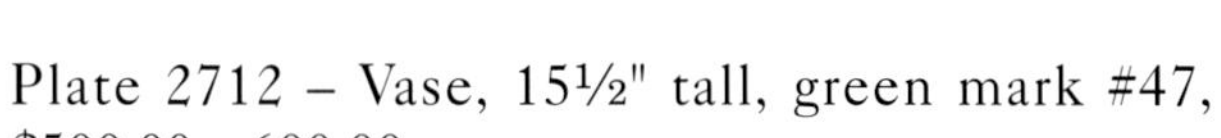

Plate 2712 – Vase, 15½" tall, green mark #47, $500.00 – 600.00.

Plate 2713 – Vase, 16¼" tall, green mark #47, $750.00 – 850.00.

Plate 2714 – Vase, 10¾" tall, blue mark #38, $250.00 – 325.00.

Plate 2715 – Vase, 10¼" tall, blue mark #52, $250.00 – 325.00.

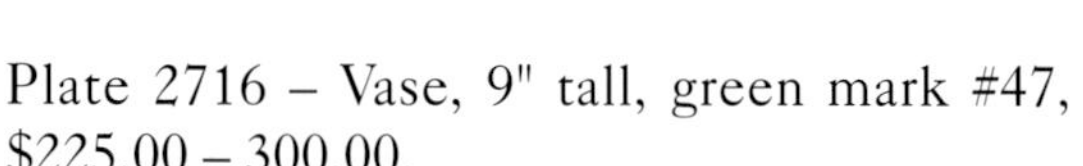

Plate 2716 – Vase, 9" tall, green mark #47, $225.00 – 300.00.

Plate 2717 – Vase, 8½" tall, blue mark #47, $250.00 – 325.00.

Plate 2718 – Vase, 10" tall, blue mark #47, $275.00 – 350.00.

Plate 2719 – Vase, 16¼" tall, green mark #47, $750.00 – 850.00.

Plate 2720 – Vase, 13" tall, green mark #47, $475.00 – 550.00.

Plate 2721 – Pair of vases, have rams head handles and horse and rider in medallion on collar of vase, green mark #47, $275.00 – 350.00 each.

Plate 2722 – Vase, unusual decor of kangaroos, 12" tall, blue mark #4, $250.00 – 300.00.

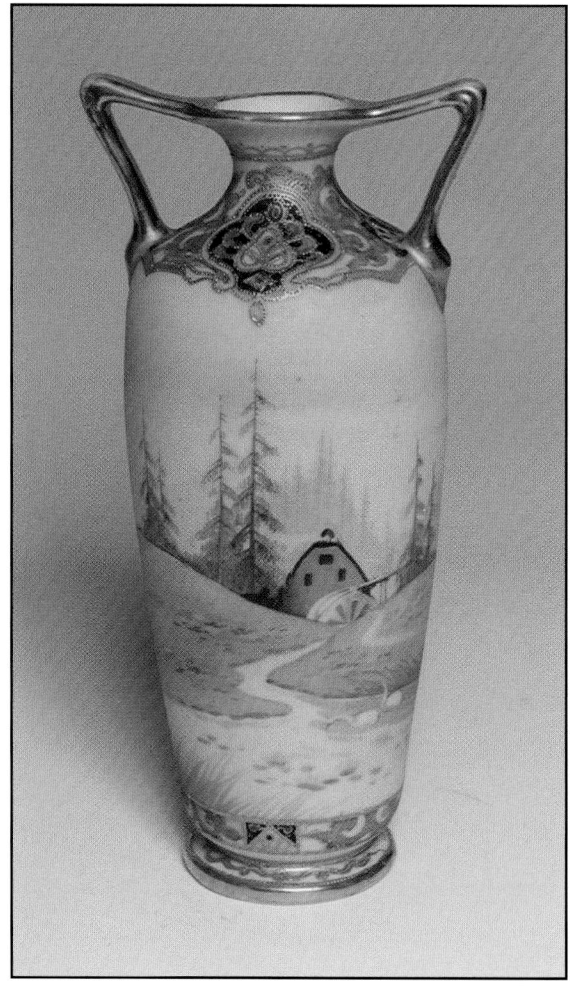

Plate 2723 – Vase, 9" tall, green mark #47, $250.00 – 300.00.

Plate 2724 – Vase, 9" tall, green mark #47, $250.00 – 325.00.

Plate 2725 – Vase, 10¾" tall, blue mark #38, $275.00 – 350.00.

Plate 2726 – Vase, 13¾" tall, green mark #47, $450.00 – 550.00.

Plate 2727 – Vase, 8¾" tall, green mark #47, $550.00 – 650.00.

Plate 2728 – Vase, 16¼" tall, green mark #47, $1,200.00 – 1,400.00.

Plate 2729 – Vase, 15" tall, green mark #47, $1,100.00 – 1,300.00.

Plate 2730 – Vase, 10" tall, blue mark #52, $350.00 – 425.00.

Plate 2731 – Vase, 12½" tall, green mark #47, $400.00 – 500.00.

Plate 2732 – Vase, 9½" tall, blue mark #43, $225.00 – 275.00.

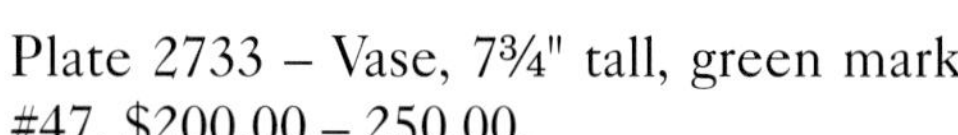

Plate 2733 – Vase, 7¾" tall, green mark #47, $200.00 – 250.00.

Plate 2734 – Vase, 10¼" tall, green mark #47, $250.00 – 300.00.

Plate 2735 – Vase, 8½" tall, green mark #47, $550.00 – 650.00.

Plate 2736 – Vase, 13" tall, green mark #47, $800.00 – 900.00.

Plate 2737 – Vase, 11" tall, green mark #47, $300.00 – 375.00.

Plate 2738 – Vase, 8" tall, blue mark #47, $325.00 – 400.00.

Plate 2739 – Vase, 7" tall, green mark #47, $225.00 – 275.00.

Plate 2740 – Vase, 11" tall, green mark #47, $325.00 – 400.00.

Plate 2741 – Vase, 11" tall, mark #38, $250.00 – 325.00.

Plate 2742 – Vase, 6" tall, green mark #47, $200.00 – 250.00.

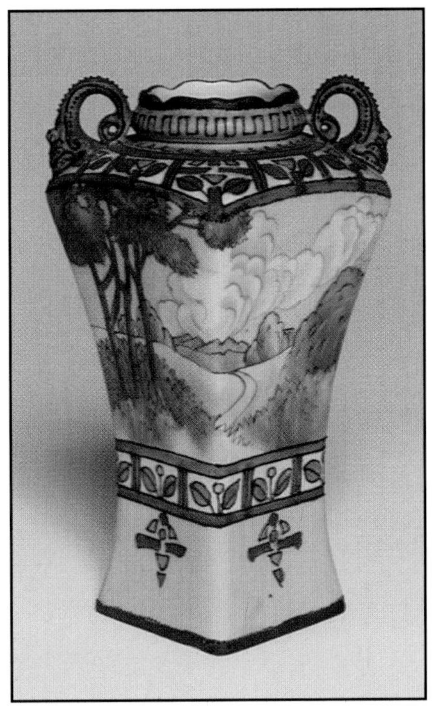

Plate 2743 – Vase, 7" tall, green mark #47, $225.00 – 275.00.

Plate 2744 – Vase, 5" tall, blue mark #52, $350.00 – 400.00.

Plate 2745 – Vase, 6¾" tall, green mark #47, $675.00 – 750.00.

Plate 2746 – Vase, 9" tall, green mark #47, $375.00 – 450.00.

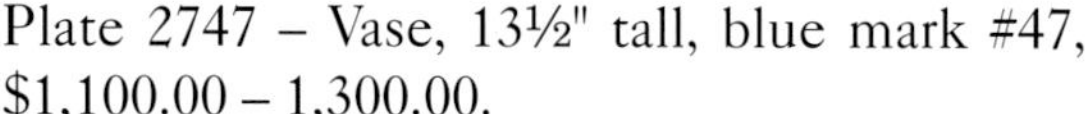

Plate 2747 – Vase, 13½" tall, blue mark #47, $1,100.00 – 1,300.00.

Plate 2748 – Vase, 13½" tall, green mark #47, $1,100.00 – 1,300.00.

Plate 2749 – Vase, 15" tall, green mark #47, $1,800.00 – 2,100.00.

Plate 2750 – Vase, 17¾" tall, green mark #47, $1,200.00 – 1,400.00.

Plate 2751 – Vase, 8" tall, green mark #47, $350.00 – 425.00.

Plate 2752 – Vase, 8" tall, green mark #47, $325.00 – 400.00.

Plate 2753 – Vase, 12" tall, green mark #47, $675.00 – 775.00.

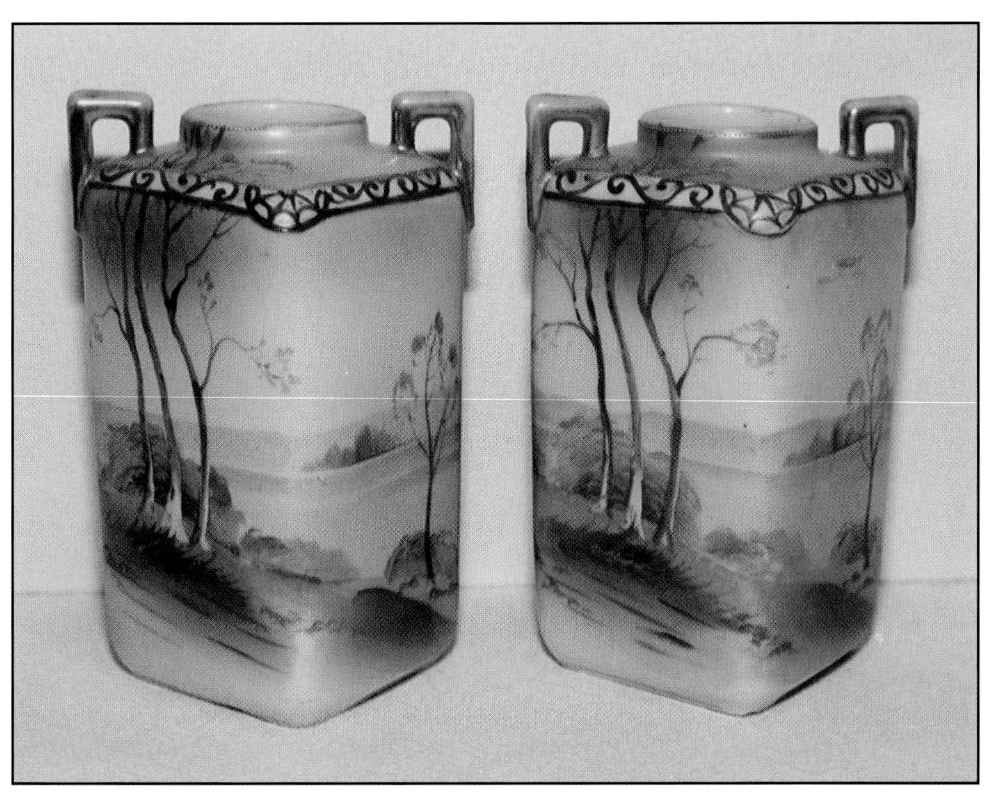

Plate 2754 – Pair of vases, 5¾" tall, blue mark #52, $200.00 – 275.00 pair.

Plate 2755 – Vase, 13" tall, green mark #47, $450.00 – 550.00.

Plate 2756 – Vase, 10" tall, green mark #47, $275.00 – 350.00.

Plate 2757 – Vase, 7¾" tall, green mark #66, $275.00 – 350.00.

Plate 2758 – Vase, 15" tall, green mark #47, $1,100.00 – 1,300.00.

Plate 2759 – Vase, 9¾" tall, green mark #47, $300.00 – 375.00.

Plate 2760 – Vase, 14" tall, green mark #47, $950.00 – 1,100.00.

Plate 2761 – Vase, 9½" tall, green mark #47, $325.00 – 400.00.

Plate 2762 – Vase, 10¼" tall, blue mark #52, $425.00 – 500.00.

Plate 2763 – Vase, 6½" tall, blue mark #3, $200.00 – 250.00.

Plate 2764 – Pair of vases, 7¼" tall, blue mark #71, $200.00 – 250.00 each.

Plate 2765 – Vase, 15½" tall, mark #239, $850.00 – 950.00.

Plate 2766 – Vase, 9¼" tall, green mark #47, $275.00 – 350.00.

Plate 2767 – Basket vase, 9" tall, green mark #47, $275.00 – 350.00. Vase, 7¾" tall, green mark #47, $275.00 – 350.00.

Plate 2768 – Wall plaque, 12¼" wide, green mark #47, $1,800.00 – 2,000.00.

Plate 2769 – Wall plaque, 12¼" wide, green mark #47, $1,500.00 – 1,700.00.

Plate 2770 – Rectangular wall plaque, artist signed K. Shinoki, 8" x 10½", green mark #47, $1,600.00 – 1,800.00.

Plate 2770A – Photo of how one collector displays this plaque in a frame.

Plate 2771 – Wall plaque, 10" wide, green mark #47, $375.00 – 425.00.

Plate 2772 – Wall plaque, 10" wide, green mark #47, $225.00 – 300.00.

Plate 2773 – Wall plaque, 10" wide, green mark #47, $300.00 – 375.00.

Plate 2774 – Wall plaque, 10" wide, blue mark #47, $325.00 – 400.00.

Plate 2775 – Wall plaque, 8" wide, blue mark #52, $225.00 – 300.00.

Plate 2776 – Wall plaque, 10" wide, green mark #47, $250.00 – 325.00.

Plate 2777 – Wall plaque, 7¾" wide, green mark #47, $250.00 – 325.00.

Plate 2778 – Wall plaque, 7¾" wide, green mark #47, $225.00 – 300.00.

Plate 2779 – Wall plaque, 9¾" wide, blue mark #52, $425.00 – 500.00.

Plate 2780 – Wall plaque, 10" wide, similar to 876, blue mark #47, $850.00 – 1,000.00.

Plate 2781 – Wall plaque, 10" wide, blue mark #52, $300.00 – 350.00.

Plate 2782 – Wall plaque, 10" wide, green mark #47, $300.00 – 350.00.

Plate 2783 – Wall plaque, 10" wide, green mark #47, $250.00 – 300.00.

Plate 2784 – Wall plaque, 10" wide, green mark #47, $350.00 – 400.00.

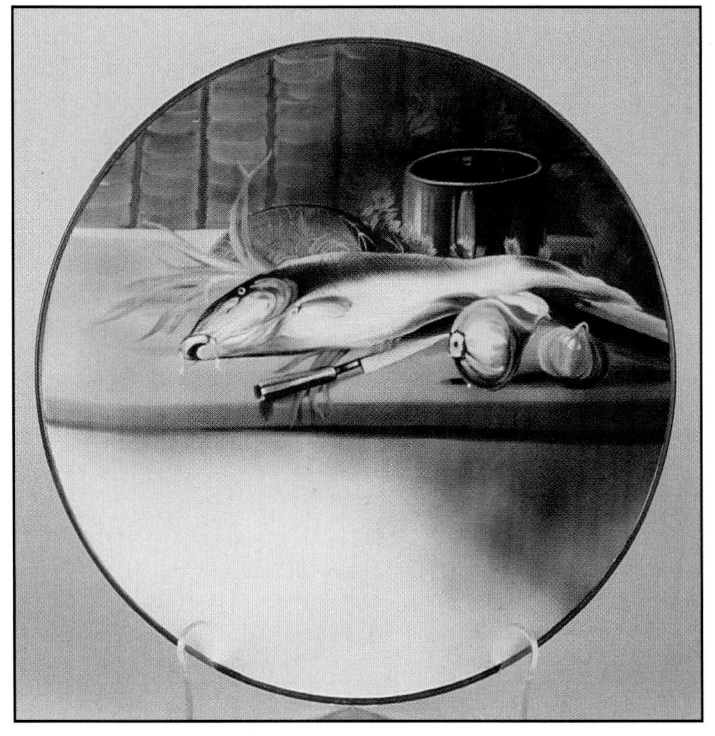

Plate 2785 – Wall plaque, 12¼" wide, green mark #47, $425.00 – 500.00.

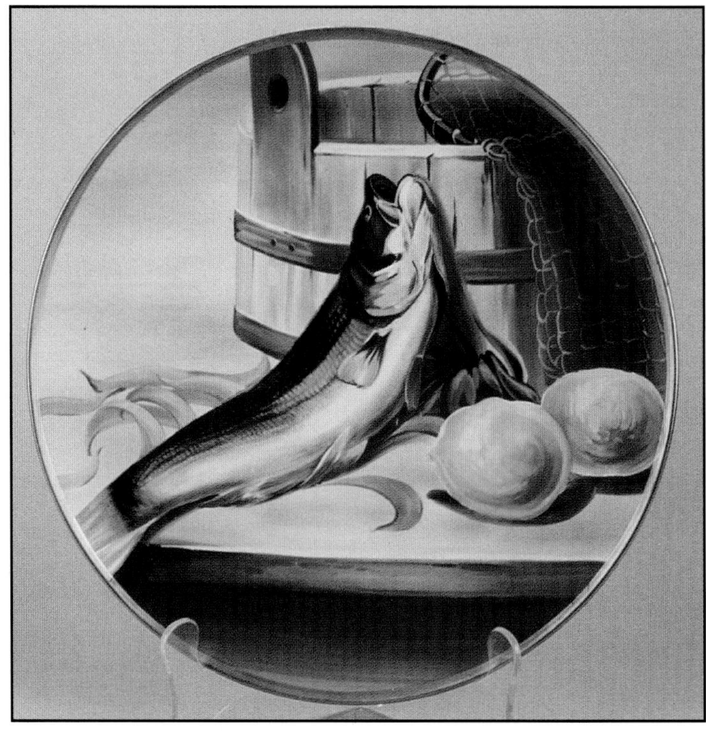

Plate 2786 – Wall plaque, 12¼" wide, green mark #47, $425.00 – 500.00.

Plate 2787 – Wall plaque, 12¼" wide, green mark #47, $425.00 – 500.00.

Plate 2788 – Wall plaque, 12¼" wide, green mark #47, $425.00 – 500.00.

Plate 2789 – Wall plaque, 10¾" wide, green mark #47, $350.00 – 400.00.

Plate 2790 – Wall plaque, 10" wide, blue mark #47, $250.00 – 325.00.

Plate 2791 – Wall plaque, 10" wide, blue mark #52, $275.00 – 350.00.

Plate 2792 – Wall plaque, 10" wide, green mark #47, $275.00 – 350.00.

Plate 2793 – Wall plaque, 10" wide, green mark #47, $350.00 – 400.00.

Plate 2794 – Wall plaque, 10" wide, blue mark #47, $300.00 – 350.00.

Plate 2795 – Wall plaque, 11" wide, green mark #47, $450.00 – 550.00.

Plate 2796 – Wall plaque, 11" wide, blue mark #47, $275.00 – 325.00.

Plate 2797 – Smoke set, tray is 10" wide, mark #47, $750.00 – 850.00.

Plate 2798 – Ashtray, 5" wide, blue mark #38, $300.00 – 375.00.

Plate 2799 – Ashtray and cigar holder, 5" wide, mark #17, $175.00 – 225.00.

Plate 2800 – Smoke set, tray is 10" wide, mark #47, $750.00 – 850.00.

Plate 2801 – Smoke set, green mark #47, $750.00 – 850.00.

Plate 2802 – Humidor, 7" tall, blue mark #47, $750.00 – 850.00.

Plate 2803 – Humidor, 6¼" tall, green mark #47, $400.00 – 500.00.

Plate 2804 – Humidor, 5½" tall, green mark #47, $550.00 – 650.00.

Plate 2805 – Humidor, 5½" tall, green mark #47, $400.00 – 450.00.

Plate 2806 – Humidor, 7¼" tall, green mark #47, $900.00 – 1,100.00. Humidor, 7¼" tall, green mark #47, $900.00 – 1,100.00.

Plate 2807 – Humidor, 7¾" tall, blue mark #52, $1,100.00 – 1,300.00. Humidor, 7¾" tall, blue mark #52, $1,100.00 – 1,300.00.

Plate 2808 – Humidor, 7" tall, green mark #47, $1,000.00 – 1,300.00.

Plate 2809 – Humidor, 7" tall, green mark #47, $850.00 – 1,000.00.

Plate 2810 – Humidor, 8" tall, green mark #47, $850.00 – 1,000.00.

Plate 2811 – Humidor, 6" tall, blue mark #38, $575.00 – 675.00.

Plate 2812 – Humidor, 7" tall, green mark #47, \$575.00 – 675.00.

Plate 2813 – Humidor, 7½" tall, green mark #47, \$1,800.00 – 2,000.00.

Plate 2814 – Humidor, 7" tall, green mark #47, \$600.00 – 700.00.

Plate 2815 – Humidor, 7" tall, green mark, #47, \$650.00 – 750.00.

Plate 2816 – Stein, 7" tall, green mark #47, $650.00 – 750.00.

Plate 2817 – Stein, 7¼" tall, green mark #47, $600.00 – 700.00.

Plate 2818 – Mug, 5" tall, green mark #47, $300.00 – 400.00.

Plate 2819 – Mug, 4½" tall, mark #47, $300.00 – 400.00.

Plate 2820 – Wine jug, 11" tall, green mark #47, $1,000.00 – 1,200.00.

Plate 2821 – Wine jug, 11" tall, green mark #47, $900.00 – 1,000.00.

Plate 2822 – Whiskey jug, 7½" tall, green mark #47, $750.00 – 900.00.

Plate 2823 – Wine jug, 11" tall, blue mark #52, $850.00 – 1,000.00.

Plate 2824 – Tankard, 10" tall, green mark #52, $500.00 – 600.00.

Plate 2825 – Tankard, 12¼" tall, mark #89, $650.00 – 750.00.

Plate 2826 – Tankard, 12½" tall, unmarked, $775.00 – 850.00.

Plate 2827 – Tankard, 16" tall, mark #50 minus the word Nippon, $750.00 – 850.00.

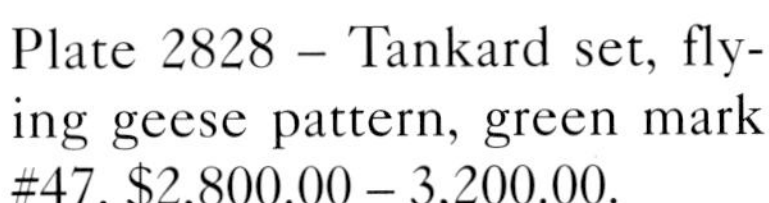

Plate 2828 – Tankard set, flying geese pattern, green mark #47, $2,800.00 – 3,200.00.

Plate 2829 – Tankard set, similar to Plate 885, tankard is 11" tall, green mark #47, $2,800.00 – 3,200.00.

Plate 2830 – Dresser set, flying geese pattern, tray is 12" long, green mark #47, $750.00 – 850.00.

Plate 2831 – Powder box and hair receiver, each 4½" wide, blue mark #52, $125.00 – 165.00 set.

Plate 2832 – Cologne bottle, 4½" tall, green mark #47, $150.00 – 200.00.

Plate 2833 – Desk set, green mark #47, $1,100.00 – 1,300.00.

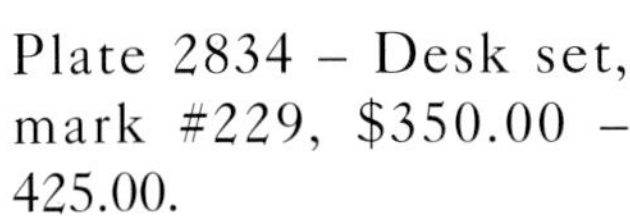

Plate 2834 – Desk set, mark #229, $350.00 – 425.00.

Plate 2835 – Chocolate set, mark #99, $850.00 – 950.00.

Plate 2836 – Chocolate set, green mark #52, $875.00 – 950.00.

Plate 2837 – Chocolate set, blue mark #52, $1,300.00 – 1,500.00.

Plate 2838 – Chocolate set, blue mark #52, $850.00 – 1,000.00.

Plate 2839 – Chocolate set, blue mark #52, $1,100.00 – 1,300.00.

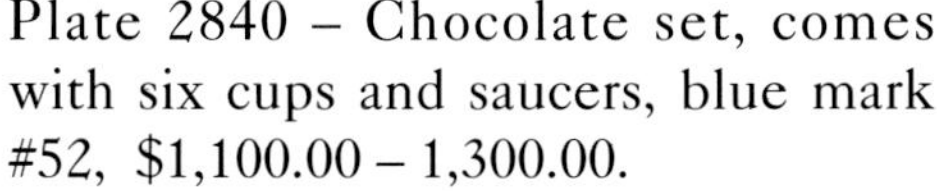

Plate 2840 – Chocolate set, comes with six cups and saucers, blue mark #52, $1,100.00 – 1,300.00.

Plate 2841 – Chocolate set, green mark #81, $950.00 – 1,100.00.

Plate 2842 – Chocolate set, green mark #52, $950.00 – 1,100.00.

Plate 2843 – Chocolate set, blue mark #52, $1,600.00 – 1,800.00.

Plate 2844 – Chocolate set, green mark #81, $1,200.00 – 1,400.00.

Plate 2845 – Chocolate set, green mark #52, $1,100.00 – 1,300.00.

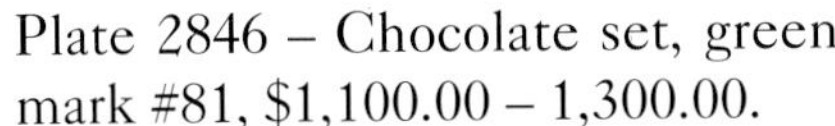

Plate 2846 – Chocolate set, green mark #81, $1,100.00 – 1,300.00.

Plate 2847 – Tea set, blue mark #52, $900.00 – 1,100.00.

Plate 2848 – Tea set, blue mark #52, $1,000.00 – 1,200.00.

Plate 2849 – Tea set, blue mark #52, $1,100.00 – 1,300.00.

Plate 2850 – Tea set, unmarked, $900.00 – 1,100.00.

Plate 2851 – Demitasse set, pot is 6¼" tall, green mark #47, $600.00 – 700.00.

Plate 2852 – Demitasse set, pot is 6½" tall, blue mark #47, $700.00 – 800.00.

Plate 2853 – Demitasse set, green mark #47, $1,300.00 – 1,500.00.

Plate 2854 – Demitasse set, flying geese pattern, geese are flying backwards on tray, green mark #47, $1,000.00 – 1,200.00.

Plate 2855 – Cake set, green mark #81, $475.00 – 550.00.

Plate 2856 – Cake set, green mark #47, $450.00 – 550.00.

Plate 2857 – Cake set, blue mark #52, $475.00 – 575.00.

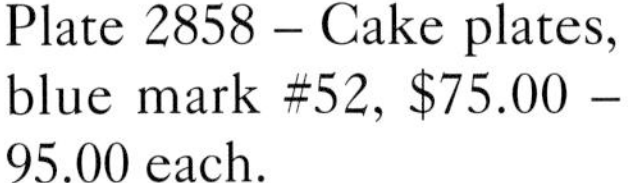

Plate 2858 – Cake plates, blue mark #52, $75.00 – 95.00 each.

Plate 2859 – Berry set, underplate is 8" wide, $250.00 – 325.00.

Plate 2860 – Platter, 16" wide, green mark #47, $750.00 – 900.00.

Plate 2860A – Close-up of platter shown in #2860.

Plate 2861 – Pitcher, 4½" tall, green mark #47, $550.00 – 650.00.

Plate 2862 – Cruet, 5½" tall, green mark #47, $225.00 – 275.00.

Plate 2863 – Pitcher, 7½" tall, green mark #47, $300.00 – 350.00.

Plate 2864 – Pitcher, 4½" tall, green mark #47, $325.00 – 375.00.

Plate 2865 – Berry set, blue mark #52, $350.00 – 425.00.

Plate 2866 – Pair of candlesticks, 7½" tall, green mark #47, $500.00 – 600.00. Ferner, 6" wide, green mark #47, $275.00 – 350.00.

Plate 2867 – Candlestick, 8¼" tall, green mark #47, $300.00 – 375.00. Pitcher, 5½" tall, green mark #47, $300.00 – 375.00.

Plate 2868 – Pair of candlesticks, 8" tall, green mark #47, $650.00 – 750.00.

Plate 2869 – Pair of candlesticks, 9½" tall, green mark #47, $750.00 – 850.00.

Plate 2870 – Cracker jar, 7¼" tall, green mark #47, $400.00 – 450.00.

Plate 2871 – Cracker jar, 8" tall, blue mark #52, $400.00 – 450.00.

Plate 2872 – Cracker jar, 9½" tall including handle, blue mark #52, $175.00 – 225.00.

Plate 2873 – Cracker jar, 6¼" tall, blue mark #47, $250.00 – 300.00.

Plate 2874 – Cracker jar, 7¾" tall, blue mark #52, $450.00 – 550.00.

Plate 2875 – Cracker jar, 8" tall, blue mark #52, $425.00 – 500.00.

Plate 2876 – Cracker jar, 7" tall, blue mark #52, $450.00 – 550.00.

Plate 2877 – Cracker jar, 8" tall, blue mark #52, $450.00 – 550.00.

Plate 2878 – Two-piece shaving mug, 3½" tall, mark #71, $300.00 – 400.00.

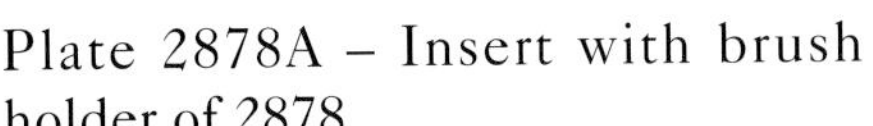

Plate 2878A – Insert with brush holder of 2878.

Plate 2879 – Sauce dish with underplate, blue mark #52, $175.00 – 225.00.

Plate 2880 – Lamp, base is 18" tall, mark unknown, $350.00 – 425.00.

Plate 2881 – Lamp, 13½" tall, blue mark #67, $1,600.00 – 1,800.00.

Plate 2882 – Salt set, tray is 10" long, green mark #47, $175.00 – 225.00.

Plate 2883 – Hostess set with matching design on box, 10½" in diameter, green mark #101, $125.00 – 165.00.

Plate 2884 – Individual coffee pot, 6" tall, blue mark #52, $125.00 – 175.00.

Plate 2885 – Reamer or juicer, 2¾" tall, blue mark #84, $125.00 – 160.00.

Plate 2886 – Trivet, 7" wide, green mark #47, $200.00 – 275.00.

Plate 2887 – Condensed milk container, blue mark #52, $150.00 – 200.00.

Plate 2888 – Condensed milk container, green mark #81, $150.00 – 200.00.

Plate 2889 – Condensed milk container, blue mark #52, $150.00 – 200.00.

Plate 2890 – Condensed milk container, green mark #52, $150.00. – 200.00.

Plate 2891 – Condensed milk container, mark #80, $150.00 – 200.00.

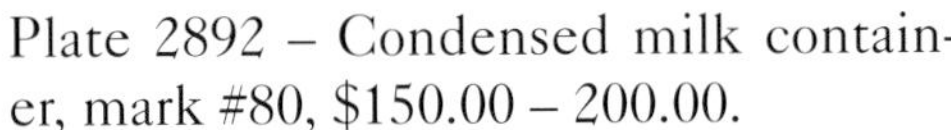

Plate 2892 – Condensed milk container, mark #80, $150.00 – 200.00.

Plate 2893 – Condensed milk container, green mark #47, $150.00 – 200.00.

Plate 2894 – Condensed milk container, green mark #47, $150.00 – 200.00.

Plate 2895 – Condensed milk container, blue mark #52, $150.00 – 200.00.

Plate 2896 – Condensed milk container, green mark #47, $150.00 – 200.00.

Plate 2897 – Condensed milk container, blue mark #89, $150.00 – 200.00.

Plate 2898 – Condensed milk container, unmarked, $150.00 – 200.00.

Plate 2899 – Doll, 21" tall, mark #249, $325.00 – 400.00.

Plate 2900 – Doll, 24" tall, mark #124, $375.00 – 450.00.

Plate 2901 – Doll, 16" tall, mark #131, $275.00 – 325.00.

Plate 2902 – Doll, 24" tall, mark #123, $375.00 – 450.00.

Plate 2903 – Doll, 18" tall, mark #127, $275.00 – 350.00.

Plate 2904 – Doll, 24" tall, mark #135, $375.00 – 450.00.

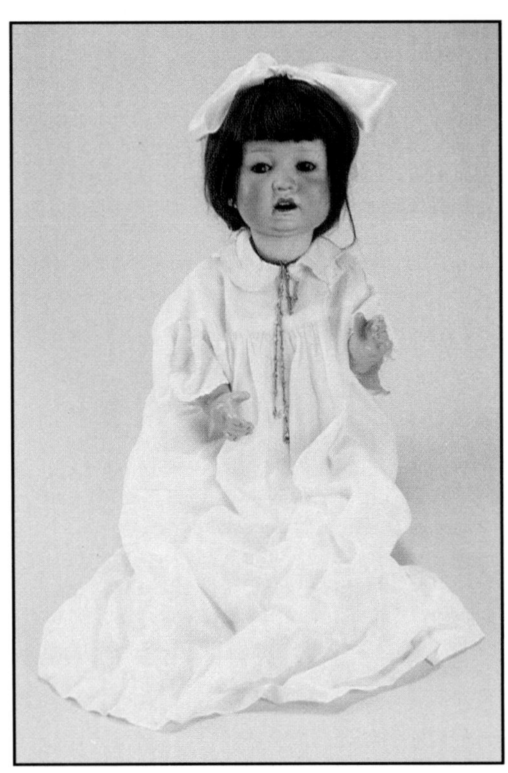

Plate 2905 – Doll, 18" tall, mark #247, $275.00 – 350.00.

Plate 2906 – Doll, 24" tall, mark #248, $375.00 – 450.00.

# GLOSSARY

American Indian design – a popular collectible in Nippon porcelain, these designs include the Indian in a canoe, Indian warrior, Indian hunting wild game, and the Indian maiden.

Apricot (ume) – in Japan, stands for strength and nobility, is also a symbol of good luck.

Art Deco – a style of decoration which hit its peak in Europe and America around 1925 although items were manufactured with this decor as early as 1910. The style was modernistic; geometric patterns were popular. Motifs used were shapes such as circles, rectangles, cylinders, and cones.

Art Nouveau – the name is derived from the French words, meaning "new art." During the period of 1885–1925, artists tended to use bolder colors, and realism was rejected. Free-flowing designs were used, breaking away from the imitations of the past.

Artist signed – items signed by the artist, most appear to be of English extraction, probably painted during the heyday of hand painting chinaware at the turn of the century.

Azalea pattern – pattern found an Nippon items, pink azaleas with green to gray leaves and gold rims. Nippon marked pieces match the Noritake marked Azalea pattern items. The Azalea pattern was originally offered by the Larkin Co. to its customers as premiums.

Backstamp – mark found on Nippon porcelain items identifying the manufacturer, exporter, or importer and country of origin.

Bamboo tree – in Japan, symbolic of strength, faithfulness, and honesty, also a good luck symbol. The bamboo resists the storm but it yields to it and rises again.

Beading – generally a series of clay dots applied on Nippon porcelain, very often enameled over in gold. Later Nippon pieces merely had dots of enameling.

Biscuit – clay which has been fired but not glazed.

Bisque – same as biscuit, term also used by collectors to describe a matte finish on an item.

Blank – greenware of bisque items devoid of decoration.

Blown-out items – this term is used by collectors and dealers for items that have a molded relief pattern embossed on by the mold in which the article was shaped. It is not actually "blown-out" as the glass items are, but the pattern is raised up from the item. (See Molded Relief.)

Bottger, Johann F. – a young German alchemist who supposedly discovered the value of kaolin in making porcelain. This discovery helped to revolutionize the china making industry in Europe beginning in the early 1700s.

Carp – fish that symbolizes strength and perseverance.

Casting – the process of making reproductions by pouring slip into molds.

Cha no yu – Japanese tea ceremony.

Chargers – archaic term for large platters or plates.

Cheese hard clay – same as leather hard clay.

Cherry blossoms – national flower of Japan and emblem of the faithful warrior.

Ching-te-Chen – ancient city in China where nearly a million people lived and worked with almost all devoted to the making of porcelain.

Chrysanthemum – depicts health and longevity, the crest of the emperor of Japan. The chrysanthemum blooms late in the year and lives longer than other flowers.

Citron – stands for wealth.

Cloisonné on Porcelain – on Nippon porcelain wares it resembles the other cloisonné pieces except that it was produced on a porcelain body instead of metal. The decoration is divided into cells called cloisons. These cloisons were divided by strips of metal wire which kept the colors separated during the firing.

Cobalt oxide – blue oxide imported to Japan after 1868 for decoration of wares. Gosu, a pebble found in Oriental riverbeds, had previously been used but was scarce and more expensive than the imported oxide. Cobalt oxide is the most powerful of all the coloring oxides for tinting.

Coralene items – were made by firing small colorless beads on the wares. Many are signed Kinran, US Patent, NBR 912171, February 9, 1909, Japan. Tiny glass beads had previously been applied to glass items in the shapes of birds, flowers, leaves, etc. and no doubt this was an attempt to copy it. Japanese coralene was patented by Alban L. Rock, an American living in Yokohama, Japan. The vitreous coating of beads gave the item a plush velvety look. The beads were permanently fired on and gave a luminescence to the design. The most popular design had been one of seaweed and coral, hence the name coralene was given to this type of design.

Crane – a symbol of good luck in Japan, also stands for marital fidelity and is an emblem of longevity.

Daffodil – a sign of spring to the Japanese.

Decalcomania – a process of transferring a wet paper print onto the surface of an item. It was made to resemble hand-painted work.

Deer – stands for divine messenger.

Diaper pattern – repetitive pattern of small design used on Nippon porcelain, often geometric or floral.

Dragons (ryu) – a symbol of strength, goodness, and good fortune. The Japanese dragon has three claws and was thought to reside in the sky. Clouds, water, and lightening often accompany the dragon. The dragon is often portrayed in high relief using the slip trailing method of decor.

Drain mold – or flopover mold, used to make flat bottomed items. Moist clay is rolled out and draped over the mold. It is then pressed firmly into shape.

Dutch scenes – popular on Nippon items, include those of windmills, and men and women dressed in Dutch costumes.

Edo – or Yedo, the largest city in Japan, later renamed Tokyo, meaning eastern capitol.

Embossed design – see molded relief.

Enamel beading – dots of enameling painted by the artist in gold or other colors and often made to resemble jewels such as emeralds and rubies. Many times this raised beading will be found in brown or black colors.

Fairings – items won or bought at fairs as souvenirs.

Feldspar – most common rock found on earth.

Fern leaves – symbolic of ample good fortune.

Fettles or Mold Marks – ridges formed where sections of molds are joined at the seam. These fettles have to be removed before the item is decorated.

Finial – the top knob on a cover of an item, used to lift the cover off.

Firing – the cooking or baking of clay ware.

Flopover mold – same as drape mold.

Flux – an ingredient added to glaze to assist in making the item fire properly. It causes the glaze to melt at a specified temperature.

Glaze – composed of silica, alumina, and flux, and is applied to porcelain pieces. During the firing process, the glaze joins together with the clay item to form a glasslike surface. It seals the pores and makes the item impervious to liquids.

Gold trim – has to be fired at lower temperatures or the gold would sink into the enameled decoration. If overfired, the

gold becomes discolored.

Gouda ceramics – originally made in Gouda, a province of south Holland. These items were copies on the Nippon wares and were patterned after the Art Nouveau style.

Gosu – pebble found in Oriental riverbeds, a natural cobalt. It was used to color items until 1868 when oxidized cobalt was introduced into Japan.

Greenware – clay which has been molded but not fired.

Hard paste porcelain – paste meaning the body of substance, porcelain being made from clay using kaolin. This produces a hard translucent body when fired.

Ho-o bird – sort of a bird of paradise who resides on earth and is associated with the empress of Japan. Also see phoenix bird.

Incised backstamp – the backstamp marking is scratched into the surface of a clay item.

Incised decoration – a sharp tool or stick was used to produce the design right onto the body of the article while it was still in a state of soft clay.

Iris – the Japanese believe this flower wards off evil; associated with warriors because of its sword-like leaves.

Jasper Ware – see Wedgwood.

Jigger – a machine resembling a potter's wheel. Soft pliable clay is placed onto a convex revolving mold. As the wheel turns, a template is held against it, trimming off the excess clay on the outside. The revolving mold shapes the inside of the item and the template cuts the outside.

Jolley – a machine like a jigger only in reverse. The revolving mold is concave and the template forms the inside of the item. The template is lowered inside the revolving mold. The mold forms the outside surface while the template cuts the inside.

Jomon – neolithic hunters and fishermen in Japan dating back to approximately 2500 B.C. Their pottery was hand formed and marked with an overall rope or cord pattern. It was made of unwashed clay, unglazed, and was baked in open fires.

Kaga – province in Japan.

Kaolin – highly refractory clay and one of the principal ingredients used in making porcelain. It is a pure white residual clay, a decomposition of granite.

Kao-ling – Chinese word meaning "the high hills," the word kaolin is derived from it.

Kiln – oven in which pottery is fired.

Leather hard clay – clay which is dry enough to hold its shape but still damp and moist, no longer in a plastic state, also called cheese hard.

Liquid slip – clay in a liquid state.

Lobster – symbol of long life.

Luster decoration – a metallic type of coloring decoration, gives an iridescent effect.

Matte finish – also referred to as mat and matt. A dull glaze having a low reflectance when fired.

McKinley Tariff Act of 1890 – Chapter 1244, Section 6 states "That on and after the first day of March, eighteen hundred and ninety-one, all articles of foreign manufacture, such as are usually or ordinarily marked, stamped, branded, or labeled, and all packages containing such or other imported articles, shall, respectively, be plainly marked, stamped, branded, or labeled in legible English words, so as to indicate the country of their origin; and unless so marked, stamped, branded, or labeled, they shall not be admitted to entry."

Meiji period – period of 1868 to 1912 in Japan when Emperor Mutsuhito reigned. It means "enlightened rule."

Middle East scenes – design used on Nippon pieces, featuring pyramids, deserts, palm trees, and riders on camels.

Model – the shape from which the mold is made.

Molded relief items – the pattern is embossed on the item by the mold in which the article is shaped. These items give the appearance that the pattern is caused by some type of upward pressure from the underside. Collectors often refer to these items as "blown-out."

Molds – contain a cavity in which castings are made. They are generally made from plaster of Paris and are used for shaping clay objects. Both liquid and plastic clay may be used. The mold can also be made of clay or rubber, however, plaster was generally used as it absorbed moisture immediately from the clay. Raised ornamentation may also be formed directly in the mold.

Moriage – refers to liquid clay (slip) relief decoration. On Nippon items this was usually done by "slip trailing" or hand rolling and shaping the clay on an item.

Morimura Bros. – importers of Japanese wares in the United States and the sole importers of Noritake wares. It was opened in New York City in 1876 and closed in 1941.

Mutsuhito – Emperor of Japan from 1868 to 1912. His reign was called the Meiji period which meant enlightened rule.

Nagoya – a large city in Japan.

Narcissus – stands for good fortune.

Ningyo – Japanese name for doll, meaning human being and image.

Nippon – the name the Japanese people called their country. It comes from a Chinese phrase meaning "the source of the sun" and sounds like Neehon in Japanese.

Noritake Co. – originally registered as Nippon Gomei Kaisha. In 1917 the name was changed to Nippon Toki Kabushiki Toki. From 1918 the word Noritake appeared in conjunction with Nippon which was the designation of country of origin.

Orchid – means hidden beauty and modesty to the Japanese.

Overglaze decoration – a design is either painted or a decal applied to an item which already has a fired glazed surface. The article is then refired to make the decoration permanent.

Pattern stamping – the design was achieved by using a special stamp or a plaster roll having the design cut into it. The design was pressed into the soft clay body of an item.

Paulownia flower – crest of the empress of Japan.

Peach – stands for marriage.

Peacock – stands for elegance and beauty.

Peony – considered the king of flowers in Japan.

Perry, Matthew, Comm., USN – helped to fashion the Kanagawa treaty in 1854 between the United States and Japan. This treaty opened the small ports of Shimoda and Hakodate to trade. Shipwrecked sailors were also to receive good treatment and an American consul was permitted to reside at Shimoda.

Petuntse – clay found in felspathic rocks such as granite. Its addition to porcelain made the item more durable. Petuntse is also called china stone.

Phoenix bird – sort of bird of paradise which resides on earth and is associated with the empress of Japan. This bird appears to be a cross between a peacock, a pheasant, and a gamecock. There appears to be many designs for this bird as each artist had his own conception as to how it should look. It is also a symbol to the Japanese of all that is beautiful.

Pickard Co. – a china decorating studio originally located in Chicago. This firm decorated blank wares imported from a number of countries including Nippon.

Pine tree – to the Japanese this tree is symbolic of friendship and prosperity and depicts the winter season. It is also a sign of good luck and a sign of strength.

Plastic clay – clay in a malleable state, able to be shaped and formed without collapsing.

Plum – stands for womanhood. Plum blossoms reflect bravery.

Porcelain – a mixture composed mainly of kaolin and petuntse which are fired at a high temperature and vitrified.

Porcelain slip – porcelain clay in a liquid form.

Porcellaine – French adaptation of the word porcelain.

Porcellana – Italian word meaning cowry shell. The Chinese ware which was brought back to Venice in the fifthteenth century was thought to resemble the cowry shell and was called porcellana.

Portrait items – items decorated with portraits, many of Victorian ladies. Some appear to be hand painted, most are decal work.

Potter's wheel – rotating device onto which a ball of plastic clay is placed. The wheel is turned and the potter molds the clay with his hands and is capable of producing cylindrical objects.

Pottery – in its broadest sense, includes all forms of wares made from clay.

Press mold – used to make handles, finials, figurines, etc. A two-piece mold into which soft clay is placed. The two pieces are pressed together to form items.

Relief – molded (See Molded Relief Items).

Royal Crockery – name of Nippon pieces marked with RC on backstamp.

Satsuma – a sea-going principality in Japan, an area where many of the old famous kilns are found, and also a type of Japanese ware. Satsuma is a cream-colored glazed pottery which is finely crackled.

Slip – liquid clay.

Slip trailing – a process where liquid clay was applied to porcelain via a bamboo or rubber tube. A form of painting but with clay instead of paint. The slip is often applied quite heavily and gives a thick, raised appearance.

Slurry – thick slip.

Solid casting mold – used for shallow type items such as bowls and plates. In this type of mold, the thickness of the walls is determined by the mold and every piece is formed identical. The mold shapes both the inside and the outside of the piece and the thickness of the walls can be controlled. Solid casting can be done with either liquid or plastic clay.

Sometsuke style decoration – items decorated with an underglaze of blue and white colors.

Sprigging – the application of small molded relief decoration to the surface of porcelain by use of liquid clay as in Jasper Ware.

Sprig mold – a one-piece mold used in making ornaments. Clay is fitted or poured into a mold which is incised with a design. Only one side is molded and the exposed side becomes the back of the finished item.

Taisho – name of the period reigned over by Emperor Yoshihito in Japan from 1912 to 1926. It means "great peace."

Tapestry – a type of decor used on Nippon porcelain. A cloth was dipped into liquid slip and then stretched onto the porcelain item. During the bisque firing the material burned off and left a textured look on the porcelain piece resembling needlepoint in many cases. The item was then painted and fired again in the usual manner.

Template – profile of the pattern being cut.

Throwing – the art of forming a clay object on a potter's wheel.

Tiger (tora) – a symbol of longevity.

Transfer print – see Decalcomania.

Translucent – not transparent but clear enough to allow rays of light to pass through.

Ultra violet lamp – lamp used to detect cracks and hidden repairs in items.

Underglaze decoration – this type of decoration is applied on bisque china (fired once), then the item is glazed and fired again.

Victorian age design – decor used on some Nippon pieces, gaudy and extremely bold colors used.

Vitreous – glass-like.

Vitrify – to change into a glasslike substance due to the application of heat.

Wasters – name given to pieces ruined or marred in the kiln.

Water lilies – represents autumn in Japan.

Wedgwood – term used to refer to Nippon pieces which attempt to imitate Josiah Wedgwood's Jasper Ware. The items generally have a light blue or green background. The Nippon pieces were produced with a slip trailing decor however, rather than the sprigging ornamentation made popular by Wedgwood. White clay slip was trailed onto the background color of the item by use of tubing to form the pattern.

Yamato – district in central Japan.

Yayoi – people of the bronze and iron culture in Japan dating back to 300-100 B.C.E. They were basically an agricultural people. They made pottery using the potter's wheel.

Yedo – or Edo, the largest city in Japan, renamed Tokyo, meaning eastern capital.

Yoshihito – Emperor of Japan from 1912 to 1926. He took the name of Taisho which meant "great peace."

# Bibliography


Butler Bros. catalogs – 1906, 1907, 1908, 1910, 1912, 1913, 1914, 1915, 1916, 1917, 1918, 1919

Gaston, Mary Frank. *The Collector's Encyclopedia of RS Prussia*. Paducah, KY: Collector Books, 1982.

Hassrick, Royal. *Northern American Indians*. London: Octopus Books Limited, 1974.

Hodge, Frederick Webb. *Handbook of American Indians*. New York City, NY: Pageant Books, 1959.

Josephy, Alvin M. Jr. (editor in charge). *The American Heritage Book of Indians*. American Heritage Publishing Co. Inc, 1961.

Josephy, Alvin M. Jr. *The Indian Heritage of America*. New York City, NY: Bantam Books, 1968.

LaFarge, Oliver. *A Pictorial History of the American Indian*. New York City, NY: Crown Publishers, 1956.

Manning Bowman Catalogs #65 and #70

Marquis, Arnold. *A Guide to American Indians*. University of Oklahoma Press, 1974.

Samuels, Peggy and Harold. *Remington the Complete Prints*. New York City, NY: Crown Publishers Inc. 1990.

Utley, Robert M. *The Lance and the Shield*. New York City, NY: Henry Hold and Co., 1993.

Van Patten, Joan F. *The Collector's Encyclopedia of Nippon Porcelain*. Paducah, KY: Collector Books, 1979.

___. *The Collector's Encyclopedia of Nippon Porcelain, Series II*. Paducah, KY: Collector Books, 1982.

___. *The Collector's Encyclopedia of Nippon Porcelain, Series III*. Paducah, KY: Collector Books, 1986.

___. *Price Guide for Collector's Encyclopedia of Nippon Porcelain, No. 3*. Paducah, KY: Collector Books, 1994.

Viola, Herman J (general editor). *Sitting Bull*. Milwaukee, WI: Raintree Publishers, 1990.

Yates, Diana. *Chief Joseph*. Staten Island, NY: Ward Hill Press, Staten Island Press, 1992.


# Index

# Schroeder's ANTIQUES Price Guide

. . . is the #1 best-selling antiques & collectibles value guide on the market today, and here's why . . .

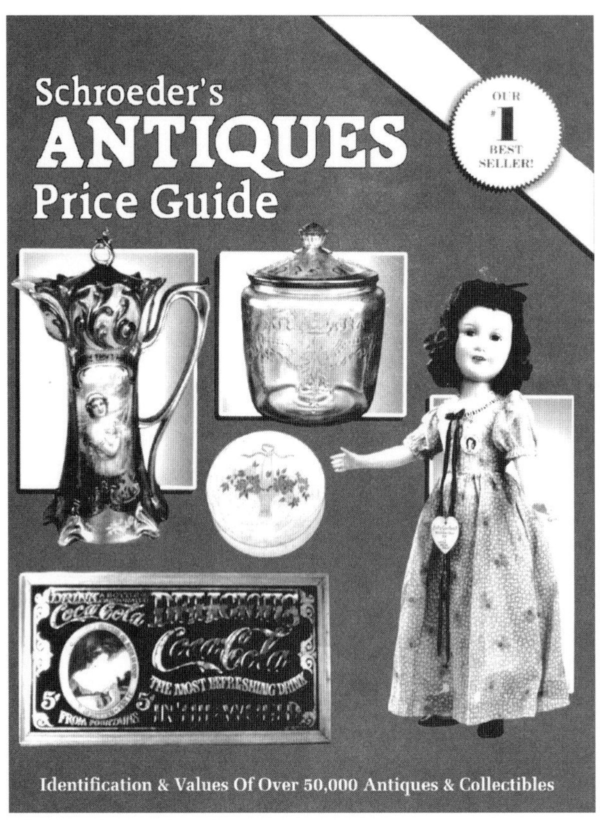


***8½ x 11, 608 Pages, $12.95***

*• More than 300 advisors, well-known dealers, and top-notch collectors work together with our editors to bring you accurate information regarding pricing and identification.*

*• More than 45,000 items in almost 500 categories are listed along with hundreds of sharp original photos that illustrate not only the rare and unusual, but the common, popular collectibles as well.*

*• Each large close-up shot shows important details clearly. Every subject is represented with histories and background information, a feature not found in any of our competitors' publications.*

*• Our editors keep abreast of newly developing trends, often adding several new categories a year as the need arises.*

---

If it merits the interest of today's collector, you'll find it in *Schroeder's*. And you can feel confident that the information we publish is up to date and accurate. Our advisors thoroughly check each category to spot inconsistencies, listings that may not be entirely reflective of market dealings, and lines too vague to be of merit. Only the best of the lot remains for publication.

Without doubt, you'll find
SCHROEDER'S ANTIQUES PRICE GUIDE
the only one to buy for
reliable information and values.

**COLLECTOR BOOKS**
***A Division of Schroeder Publishing Co., Inc.***